Letters for Origin

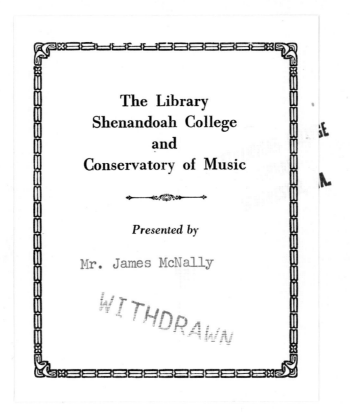

CHARLES OLSON

Letters for Origin

1950-1956

Edited by Albert Glover

Cape Goliard Press
in Association with Grossman Publishers New York 1970

Copyright © *Charles Olson 1969*

This first edition has been designed,
printed and published by Cape Goliard
Press, 10A Fairhazel Gardens, London
N.W.6.

The publishers wish to thank The Academic
Center Library, The University of Texas,
for their permission to reproduce these
letters.

U.K. SBN: p. 206 61757 7; c. 206 61756 9
L. of C. No. 75 93577

Printed in the U.S.A.

Second Printing

To Cid Corman, Editor

Wed Oct 18   50   217 Randolph Pl   NE   Wash 2 DC

My dear Cid Corman:
                        It took me a bit, but you must not mind: we had
our lad, to keep us in touch. . . .

                        Well, the thing you ought to know, is, that, that
you have the will to make a MAG is a very fine thing, and is hailed, by
this citizen, (especially, I suppose, that it is also BOSTON: by god,
how long is it, that except for harvard sheets, which is not boston, there
has been SUCH A THING!   all the way back to Emerson's DIAL, i do
declare, almost, isn't it?   We except, of course, the quality, even when
it was edited by WDHowells!)
                        Good for you. And may it prosper.
                                                        Now that
sounds as tho I did not also welcome yr suggestion, yr OFFER, that I
join you, as CONTRIB ED.   Not at all.   On the contrary.   Smells mighty
good.   But I am an older animal.   And smell thrice, as I go around a new
baby, just, to make sure, it's going to be, a—as I was—had to be shook—
to be mighty sure, there's breath BREATH in it.   (That shake must be
why I got to be 6′7, oi dare soy.)

It comes to this: any dispersing of authority means dispersing of force.
Which, in our terms, means TASTE, or however one puts JUDGMENT,
on poem, story, any prose or form known to man.
                                        Now you've had the
will—and so, already, you give a poem of mine (2 poems) a bed to go
to to find print.   You have taken the step.   It is a proud one, for the likes
of me.   I am immensely grateful, that you exist.   OK.
                                        Look: so far, in
my short experience (that is, as writer) I have found only one man who
has JUDGMENT in these matters the equal of what I take to be the DEMAND
of our going reality.   That lad you know.

                                Let me put it, straight, and
strong.   Have you already asked any others (beside Creeley) to be such
secondary editors? Answer me that one, friend, and I'll come up with
a possible suggestion.   Okay?

Let me hear fr you, and now, that it is going, you'll not have to wait,
for answers.   I wanted to unload this bomb, on the 1st run. . . .

I

Monday Oct 21 50   [217 Randolph Pl Washington]

My dear C Corman:
                That's okay. I think yr reasons are wrong BUT
the piece ["The Gate and the Center"] is not yet set, so please *don't*
send it to anyone until, inside the family, we have put it right. And I'll
tell you why: because, THIS piece is a testing (TESTING) not only of
possible fresh new form in yr MAG but also test of how free you are
going to be, my new friend!

                Take it step by step, thus: (1) the moment I learned
(fr Ferrini, then you, then the Creel) that you were prepared to push by
me the IDEA of correspondence not as of a notable but as a THING in
itself (a FORM, UNFORM), a via of person pushing, then, I sd, this
weekend, the right thing to do with G & C, is to break it back either (1)
to its first form as solid (most of the Waddell adds out) or (2) to let it
emerge as of a lot of other slugs of letters before and aft, so that, its
moving, will find place in larger notions, & thus, its jags can be left,
with other pieces, on each side, to make elaborations or clarities of
frame:

                for ex., yr objections to my slugging EDUC (not ERE) are founded
on not-yet-sufficient-knowledge of primary position)the poet is the
pedagogue left(now don't kid yrself: (1) je suis un ecolier—and why
not? (Cf, below, on this, as of art, now, here, USA, and yr problems,
as of same scholarship vs traditional verse or mag concepts) (2) I am
long experienced in those places where ONE IS NOT LED OUT   (3) One
cannot exaggerate the dangers, given contemp.(t) mags, and general
control (CONTROL) of culture by, not scholars, but academics (which
is practicing poets, I mean, & critics, not, not, not SCHOLARS—(you
are sucking wind with yr arse when you take it, I use names, hollowly
(names of men so selected become images of force not taken up, my
barbarous bostonian)

                    (CONTROL: and by MONEY, my poor confronted lad: don't
                    think I don't know all those arguments (what the hell do
                    you think I've been doing trying to earn a living all these
                    years: don't preach to me, the cons: I not only know them
                    but have been executive several times over, and know
                    (AND PASS BY, my lad) these false necessities

                        Just this. Please don't argue
          Brandeis, or 10,000 dollars olson-side. I have, my
          friend (and we'll go to details on this, any time you say),
          PASSED UP more of such dough in short-mid-long life
          (and from your own very sources, like kind, several

planes, in this hyar economy) than you are now
talking about.

          And here's the JOKER you must
learn YET: that, despite all appearances & advice
fr others (who have not had such chance or have
given in) the TIME HAS COME when they need US,
and you can play it STRONG, boy: can play it STR.

    (As a matter of fact, yr own somewhat surprised ex-
pression that there *is* backing, is proof—(what I
like is, that *you* have proved it (MAKES A COUP
for you as pioneer (but turn it yr way (don't give me
that dangerous modesty, that the Brandeis gang are
shrewder than you—nuts, you are as shrewd as they
come   (and my job is to keep warning you not to be
too SHREWD: for that's the whole trouble

with such talent as yrs: that, other shrewd men who are already in,
make an impression on you.   Look, Cid, take it as straight & friendly:
PLAY IT STRONG, don't KNUCKLE to dough, it'll come your way
ANYWAY

    (The fact that you have gone so far with R CR, and am now
willing, despite nervousness, to take a 40 page plunge
with Olson, is plenty proof, you are no willy

                       And we'll
see you thru.   Don't be nervous.   I'm ready to whack you

the best 40 pages of, olson YET.   And sure nuf R CR, as 2nd no.,

is as sure a bet as you can put that MONEY on, this lad, he, is

So, to get back, and on:

(1)   you have stomach, and say, in this letter to me this morning,
     I WILL USE G & C.   That's straight, and good.   And it will shake
     down, the moment we have the correspondence section worked out:
     (even the anglo-saxon will get into place, be cool abt that!)

(2)   you have two poems, now.   If you will give me some notion of date
     you will appear, I will slate work in hand (verse) so that all that is
     top will go to you.   (In fact, right now, I could lay home to you

3

poems done since spring which would make anthology out &
ahead of what has been done.)   My only wish is that you will
lead the Olson section in, with the verse.   Or maybe, to keep
the whole IDEA as fresh as possible, start with a verse, and
then break in with prose, and then out, again to verse.   Or some
such ordering, as of the way the *process* is.   (We should be able
to organize such a thing together most alively.   Just let me know
date, and guarantee me such space to push with, and I'll give it
to you, hot.)

(3)   The possibility of a story is one which I will take up later.

Okay?   (Only jesus christ, don't tell me I'll do better: don't you yet
know a man knows more abt what he hasn't done, isn't doing,
than any other man sitting out there with a beady eye?)

All right.   Now I want to go further with yr whole idea (and i do it, not
to stick my finger back in yr eye, at all (figured to do this anyway), but
in order that i may function for you as *sluice of other men's work* for
you and to you: REMEMBER THAT

For example.   There is one Robert Barlow sitting down there in Atzcapotzalco.   I want you to tell me if you ever heard of him.   (Or, for that
matter, did you ever hear of Sauer?)   (Or, for that matter, right down
yr street, one Merk—Frederick Jackson Merk?)   Please tell me.   For
it will make the point, without derogation to you at all.   Just, clarities,
en scene.
           (I was deeply disturbed by yr remark (2nd last letter) that you
           would expunge fr my letters all remarks but those on art!)

Let me try to put the whole thing in one package.   (You won't be able to
show this letter to Brandeis, but by god if such a conception of a MAG
as herein drawn is *not* more pertinent to them than some dishwater
aesthetic flag flying from their masthead, I have wasted my time trotting
up and down this land like Johnny Appleseed (and precisely in their well-
heeled gardens with serpentine walls, as Mr Tom J had the perception
to bound them by!)

                    (I *am* the wandering scholar, you dope.)
                    And paid, bro, and PAID!

You see, the pay-off is, that it is, actually, precisely, what you think is

a way of making me burn.   It is, god help me, a question of,
KNOWLEDGE—this business, of, how you, Cid Corman, can, 1951,
construct a MAG, which will be pumpkins.

Now I'll try to say HOW.   First, grab hold of this PRINCIPLE, you are
already pushing: the correspondence as well as the finished work of,
men (that finished work, of course, in the case of olson being, obviously,
"finished" by same process of bearing in, on, toward, as is the so-called
un-finished.)

    1—it has nothing to do, actually, with olson: it has to do
      with a process of *fronting* to the *whole* front of reality
      as it now presents itself

    2—it rests (such a 40 pages, *with* correspondence) on a
      premise that no such confrontation can be done
      by
      (a) the old deductive premise of form—and that
        goes for *poems* as well as *essays* as well as
        stories (mark you)

      (b) that art & culture are somehow separated fr
        the other planes of energy on which a people
        express themselves (economics, politics,
        films, television, or whatever "entertainment")

      (c) that life (what is "human") is an absolute in-
        stead of—what I think I am not at all alone in
        taking it—that is, specifically, "Life", that
        dirty capital (doric, corinthian OR iambic)—
        IS RELATIVE to conditions of REALITY (as
        distinguished from, as *ahead* of life "human
        life", at any given time::: life, in this sense, is
        a stop to consolidate gains already being pushed
        beyond by the reality instant to you or to any man
        who is *pushing*

OK.   Now why do you agree with R CR, that most of the stuff in the MAGS
you read is (I won't use your careless scatology) ?   Why?   (Or why do I
find so many of the writers whom you are impressed by, decidedly *im-*
pressive for their sometimes extreme talents, well-made poems, stories,
pieces——o, say, Harvey Shapiro, or Richard Wilbur, or Miss Hoskins,
or, Stephen Spender (intimate) or who else do you think of publishing?)

WHY?   And why should I weep to see you get out only another of such
MAGS as Hudson, or PNY, or NINE?
          (Why do such make so much of the

literary inheritance?   Why do you get, not only in the so-called creative work enclosed but also in the STATEMENTS (Russell's, say, announcing, that magic no., 9) such overt, coy, or covert woooing of—by adjectives, by flaccid praising—exclusively *art* or *literate* precedecessors?

Is there not a direct connect between the emphasis on (1) technical, skill and (2) tradition—that is, cultural tradition—the *assumption* of a sure-human core: "hoomin", I mean (and not al clapp's clear objection) : which is, was, always is, LIKE:

a connect between this, and the "O, I am here, and O, I am human, and O, isn't it, weary-or-howlyrically lovely" (Barbara Gibbs) or "o not pretty yet but will be" (Rukeyser or the lazy leftists) or "it stinks, because, tho i don't say, I stink, which is what humans always have done, look at Diogenes" or any of same, which you may document, even on such a high level (so much a source as) T.S. (GI) Eliot?

Which accomplisheth WHAT (where are we at this 40 yr end of that essay "Tradition & the Individual Talent"?   Of the *whole* LITTEL MAG (exception: the drive of EP—who never for a moment let his hand slip off the Johnson rod to his own loco., HIS energy as the thing to be put to USE by ANYTHING of the past—never let the PAST for its own sake ("human positionalism") slide him off   (well, could say things otherwise here, but, in context, he and WCW, only, ONLY, mind you, excuse what is now HUDSON   PNY KENYON   etc. — or why do you think it is only those two men whom they are able to sell their sheets by?
(now it is Melville, yes: but, what a Melville—the same bizness, turn him into that same g.d. human humus, because, "we, poor things, have to have *soil* to grow *skillfull* in"
SHIT
THE PRESENT GOING REALITY IS THE ONLY SUCH SOIL

All right, with that last CAP STATEment, let's go to yr MAG

do you, cid corman, think that you can put out a PUSH, now, by not following up on the FIRST PRINCIPLE (the non-deductive, but formal totality of a man, say, in each issue) to the SECOND PRINCIPLE, the same, from p. 1.   to page 75 (you say)
AS OF THE WHOLE REALITY NOW?

do you think you can get that in by an eclectic selection of aesthetic work around these States—and, as you make me so nervous by—by similar selection from the WOILD?

okay—there is barlow. what's he doing, that interests me? His main job,
right now, is a life of Montezuma. He has edited for some years a LITTLE
MAG called Tlluocan—in, watch this, NAHUATL. The last thing of his I
saw was two pages in "Circle"—one a drawing by him of a "madonna" of
rocks and a spring he discovered in Oaxaca or somewhere. The other page
was his impeccable and discriminating description of where he found it and
what it is. (He also writes verse, the quality of which, I cannot speak of.)

Some years ago a writer named Resnikoff published a little book called
TESTIMONY. He is a lawyer. He made his book up of selections from
court records, or situations, or words, or "plots" therein discovered.

Diana Woellfer (wife of Emerson Woellfer, Chicago Painter) sent me
Saturday a cat. of SIX STATES PHOTOGRAPHY (Milwaukee Museum).
Her own photo was of kids under swinging door of cantina (very much
Cartier-Bresson :::: if
                    I got you notes by H C-B on trip just now
                    completing self, Peking (Mao's entrance) ;
                    Shang hai (the Gang's Retreat) ; India,
                    Indonesia, and auto trip Calcutta to Paris
                    ((the sort of thing he might well do, yet
                    no one is editing in such a fashion as to
                    call him out) short notes—WOT WOULD
                    YOU DO WITH IT (alongside Theodore
                    Roethke)?

Another photo was, title: "Thiocarbamide Crystals 900 X". For years the
best prose I read was not tseliot but in work of selig hecht, clarence graham
& other physio-psychologists working on such things as the rods and cones
in a pigeon's eye. (In yr own backyard: more available example: the prose
of one Wiener, mathematician where up there? Compare to (Brandeis)
Lewisohn. (Or your own prose, MISTER corman).

I have in my hand a poem by one R CR, called, "Christmas Comes Early to
One Los Angeles Youth"—which is clippings from AP story out of LA, mit
comments, including "phew!"

One Paul Valery, when he did edit a magazine, called it—look!—
COMMERCE . . .

7

WHAT SELECTIVE PRINCIPLE IS THERE, the equal of, GETTING IN

THE GOING ENERGY OF THIS PRESENT—here and now, US, 1951—

for A MAG?

((is yr "taste" in prose or verse—or mine (on *quality* level) as in-
TERESTING?   as IMPORTANT as an attempt to do just that?
                                                         TO GIVE
IT, AS FAR AS YOUR LIMITS GO, not taste, but ENERGY?

                                        is an editor NOW
as recorder of such not much more important than, an editor, as

lyric soul?   as critic?   as eclectic collector of friends, etc., as

LITERARY WORK?

I don't think, this day, or you, at this stage as correspondent, is getting
my heat up enuf to make the points which should be made.   BUT do you
know what started me on this track?   You did.   When you wrote abt "foreign"
material, to me or Cree.   I don't remember which.

Look: any French writer (say, better than Michaux, or Eluard, for our
                        purpose right now, Remy de Gourmont, say)
        stands on SCHOLARSHIP of his people (as well as a clear tradition
        back thru the Latin to the Greek and on back)

        he can be interlacktuwal as all hell *because* he has a body of
        work which he and his readers take for granted, base themselves
        on (a culture breathes, takes breath for granted, as men do)

        but such breath has been worked for, milleniums, my lad

DO YOU HONESTLY THINK—or know, for that matter—ANY AMERICAN
CAN GO ON SUCH ASSUMPTION?
                                Have you *any* sanctions for your acts?
                                Even for editing a MAG?

But take a look at any little mag, take a look at the PNY issue starring
Apollinaire.
                What happens?   The oldest thing here in these States:
backtrailing, colonialism, culture scratching!

                                Suddenly Bill Merwin, or
whoever is alongside, is, shown up, to be proceeding on culture concepts—

8

humanisms—which are patently NOT HIS
                                And with no such CORE
of ENERGY to offset same fine flowering of PAST: What happens?
                                mag collapses, as FORCE

PNY, that issue, was, nothing but reprint of APOLLINAIRE—which, by
god, any alert man would have gone to, at source, as part of process of
learning his trade in this hear time & day (or to some equivalent of same—
as Rimbaud, say, or Edgar Allen Poe (as WCW mined him, *not* Baudelaire)

You see, it isn't at all a matter of jingoism.   It is quite another thing.   It
is, this proposition: the reality contemporary to us, here, in the States
(remember, you are publishing, Boston, 1951) is the thing we are offered
by which to gauge reality.   (The other thing, human, is, (the gauge is) of
course, our own selves (which, by the way, is the reason, *not any other*,
why, the limits I spoke of above, remain: you will, of course, set out to,
print, creative work.   You are not trying to cover the sociology.   Or the
politics.   Or the economics.   Or the "literature".   You are seeking to
express, by a selection of work afoot by writers, what is—as far as you
can get it in—the going reality culture-wise.   Right?

BUT ask yrself: how, in a people and country like the US, 1951, does
reality culture-wise express itself *at its top*?

                                Do you for a moment think
it will express itself as FRANCE did?   Or Russia?   Or Japan, now, 1951?
Not to speak of Athens, 450 BC

Is the American energy (I am not local: I am playing this record against
a background of events already played out: the Americanization of the
world, now, 1950: soda pop & arms for France to fight, not in Europe, but
in Indo China, the lie of it)

                    is that energy—where do you find it ex-
pressed?   In the fiction of RPWarren?
                                In the poems of BILL merwin?

Look, one of the reasons why I stress American scholarship (note bene,
Brandeis)
            Sauer   Barlow   Stefansson   Lattimore   Porada (think she's
                                                Italian, actually)
Wiener   Edgar Anderson   (on maize in Assam)

9

IS,   that the American PUSH is not at all   all machines & engineers

THE FACT is, that, americans are putting out a body of research ROUND
the WORLD, which is the kind of grounding on which that culture of Europe
rested rests is now buried in here lies the anthill

why not pick up, see, make clear, illuminate WHAT's UP (as well as
discover another Ezra Pound or—well, since Melville—who wrote prose)

why not (what does it matter that, Sauer, say, only publishes in Am Philo
Soc mags: is not yr job (and mine as helper) to DOCUMENT that PUSH?

KNOWLEDGE, lad, is what art and culture BUILD ON

            well, i quit, for now.   Another time, another time.   Maybe
it comes to this:
                    if you are already ready to put one man forward
                    in his (approximate) totality—give a shot at
                    his reach by way of fragments and putsches,
                    go by spontaneous, irregular, guerilla forms;

                    why not take this the step further it already
                    implies, and make that the form of your MAG:
                    make it, such a presentation, a RE ENACTMENT OF,

                    the going reality of (approximate, shot at) THAT
                    WHICH IS ABREAST OF US: now, here & now, *not*
                    what was what was we do lament

                    THE WHOLE FRONT, not "culture"   "art"   (I note
                    PNY, in announcing next issue, says "exciting new
                    poets" SHIT)   "creative work" (thus admitting,
                    furthering, the whole separateness and classifications
                    which logic & positivism (as well as Xty & Hebraism)
                    have fostered)   the whole dull business of CULTURE

look—a creative man is, 1st, an alive one, and, as alive, takes care
of his business, including his skills, or he's not alive, not creative, and
not worth the waste of yr attention

                            we are not here either to
praise or to bury BUT TO EXAMINE

what's around, that is of USE, not that, we admire:

AESTHETICS   pah   bah   shit   (leave that to what already is—*all* mags
                                     now existent in Am And Eng, so far as
                                     I can see)

       give us something actually NEW, mr cc, and the EX-

       CITING, will take care of itself   (believe me, bro.)

A GRAPH:

       ENERGY   vs   humanism

    non-deductive   vs   deduc (educ, polituck, cultchuck

NATURE TAKES NOTHING BUT LEAPS   worseus   progress, accumulation,
       (de Broglie brothers)   succession, tradition

art as the wedge of the
    WHOLE FRONT   (god help us)   vs   art as culture

                 see you another time

thurs
nov 9
50 [217 Randolph Pl   Washington]

my dear duckweed:

each sentence you write breaks my heart.   it is
as simple as that.   so let's be practical:

(1)   can you, will you, by some means (even a notary, maybe!) give me
absolute assurance you will (despite all weathers, fair or foul) give me
the 40 pages of issue ♯1 you have told me you plan to give me?

Now this is not at all to arrogate away from you any control whatsoever.   But such a deal takes *composing*.   And I cannot throw
myself forward into it if it is in any danger of wastage.   (You will
see how, it is, almost, like a book, such a block, and yet, the beauty
of it, is, it is not a book, it is a magazine, and does, therefore,
allow, precisely, the sort of composing by discontinuity, non-deduction,
field, fragment, grit & vulgarity, that, at root, can make a magazine,
today, fresh.

If you could make me confident that this part of yr 1st issue is
definite, and decided, I am most anxious to go ahead, to see the
work done and the work ahead in some such pattern, and, at a
time (I asked you, approximately when you expect to go to bed)
present it to you sufficiently ahead of the lock-up for you to go
over all stuff in those pages.

(You see, you make me very nervous, when you list the poets you
have for issue ♯1—and put down Olson (2), Creeley (1), etc.
That's the old game, 1st of all.   And 2nd, those two poems don't
go together at all: either there shld be one (MAX) or more, either
or.   And if there are more—40 pages would seem to include more,
no?—then (with letters, & such a piece as Gate & Center), there
is composing—juxtaposition, correlation, interaction—called for.)

But now I come to the HOT—that is, I can come to it if you are able to
make your decision stick, to give me the 40 pages,—that is, stick on
my most willing skin (they call me, Sticky-Hair, out there, in the woods,
where the oak is hospitable to the mistletoe). ((Boston is, where my
TrueLove. . . .))

I have this PROPOSITION, to offer, as of 50 PAGES
_____

_____

what would be much better than this one man (what could almost be
anonymous, the work issuing in its course, and, by that work alone
the men be known) is this hot:

                              50 pages to be a movement, a composing fr
the shifting correspondence of two writers, poems and stories coming up
in the progress of that correspondence, the nature of it also representing
examinations of what key points on the whole front of life & work today
that correspondence gets to

it could be an immense business—and not necessarily, be you reminded,
because of the two men involved (i am thinking of your readership and
what such an intimate, moving, upshooting thing as this would be for them,
in the pages of, a MAG, coming, new, to their hands).

But the two men involved, thank yr stars, are important, simply, because
they are serious characters whom you can well, yourself, put your pages
in the hands of!   (I say this, of course, because you have made it possible
for me to say it, that is, you have assured Creeley and myself that, the
two of us, are central to, your conception of, the MAG.)

      (Which, of course, does bring up all you write me, in yr
      two letters received today, about BRANDEIS.   But I am
      here most practical: the *test* you are looking for, of
      such censorship as Lewisohn, Hindus and Elder Gerard,
      is, precisely these 50 pages, NOT, the first year of yr
      editorship.   For you will put yrself in the position of
      earning their approval, if you go by this 1st year test:
      and it will mean, inevitably, that you will *woo* it, that
      first year.   Which, my friend, is *worse* than outright
      censorship.

      No, the thing to do, is, to pitch an act at them, to measure
      them.   (And if you want to do that right away, I am sure,
      that both Creeley and I would pour it on, to prepare, as
      rapidly as possible, those 50 pages, for you to use, as
      TEST.)

      Say the word, on this face of the thing, and the two of
      us will plunge, and present you, with, a MEASURE.

I have this feeling: you have to take up your confidence in these two men—
in their *practical* power as well as in their (yr own word, & title) creative—
now, right now, pitched as you are between (essentially) them, and the
Brandeis Board—the leetle Soupreme Curt.

13

It is always that way: you call yrself the CREATIVE QUARTERLY. If it is to be so, then, you (or anyone) is required to—to let it be "creative"— to let it come alive, be, yrself, willing to put yr faith in, life, the bitch, the confronting one.

And it is not ever, just, yr *own* notions: the pitch is no longer Corman versus Brandeis. It is, the material of, the men of, his magazine (like you say)

(like you say, eh?)

Well, that's yr problem. All I care to do, is to offer you, a THING: 50 pages of woven stuff from the heads & hands of two men (willing, I take it, to remain anonymous, remember—just so that the whole thing can be read as its own revelations, not, the intervention of, who are these men, but, what is this work)

There it is. Now, you tell me, whether to go ahead (1) instantly or / and (2) solidly.

I'll await yr answer.

Good luck

tuesday
november 14
   50   [217 Randolph Pl   Washington]

my dear Corman:

                So, it was that easy to smoke you out, was it?

Well, well.

        Look here: I don't at all care to be addressed in such

terms as this letter of yrs.   And I shall keep same for whoever or

whatever use, it is called for.

                      In yr first letter to me, you allowed
you did not think I needed you.   That remains quite, quite it.

    You are a great fool, Corman.   When a man—or two men—are
ready to pitch in, to throw all their work your way, and you make such
posings you drive them off, that is foolishness, big foolishness.

    You are really quite stupid.   You do not know the difference between
any of us just as writers who will *use* you and your mag to get things
published, and quite another will & drive, of some such writers who,
recognizing the deep use a magazine can be to all who read, would be
willing to go along with you in a project to put a magazine out which
would be of that kind of USE.

                You had nothing to fear, and all to gain.
That is, if you did not so palpably fear you have no taste at all.   But
where do you think taste & judgment come from?   They are *earned*, and
it is not the least wise way to earn taste than from your betters—especially,
when such are ready to give you the best of themselves.

                    But that takes a
little modesty.   I am embarrassed, by your lack of it.   Such preening,
that "the issue will be as I want it or there won't be any", is simply a
silly try to plug a space which is empty, empty, my boy.

                   Or this: "Deal
is to get the best we can: of what we want.   Along the PROJECTIVE trail."
I don't like at all such cheap use of a word of my own invention.   And,

15

secondly, why, if it is you, do you put it "we"?   And if it is "we", who is we, and what of olson's work & letters has "we" seen, eh?

It is altogether LOSS, Corman.   I have the impression you must be a most skillful operator.   Otherwise, how could you keep a radio tent show of verse going, as you have, and, on top of that, get such backing for a magazine as you seem to have pumped up.   And that's fine, that's of use.

On top of that, you have the awareness enough, to go to Creeley to take a body of stuff already in hand, and—and I can tell you I valued that— invite olson to take over 40 pages of your first issue.

Put those two accomplishments together, and you can stand in the light, Corman, you can stand the light.   Matter of fact, you can, after a bit, when such action is made evident, stand quite clear, with a coup or two, in the history of this business.   You could even look a good deal like a couple of such fine predecessors as Margaret Anderson and Jane Heep, you could.   And you could, as they did, earn the patronage of Jim or Jill X and the confidence of—o, say, such writers as one Creeley and one, olson.

But there it is.   You think—in a flash—to have something else, that which is not so easily earned, that which you do not have and which cannot be so easily arrogated to yrself.

No, Corman.   You have yr limits, too, quite recognizable limits.

Note the shrinkage, and ask yrself—as I could ask anyone—how come?   What, other than your own fear of your own lacks, accounts for

BANG: "am offering you 40 pages 1st no."

BANG ♯2   "won't you be contributing editor"

1st DEMER   "well, no 4 letter words, &, er, ah, o, not, let us not, we can't afford, it is unnecessary, er, to attack, a.a.a., education.   And you do throw names around. . . ."

1st NEWS of HOW THE WIND BLOWS:

"olson (2 poems)"

& NOW, when his hand is called, LOOK:

"Fuck (4 letter word, exact) everything said by me to date: to you: re
mag.
FINE idea of duet (article): let's see it.   (Oh, yeah?   "article" ?)

NO assurances.

I repeat: "NO assurances".

Look, lad, get off the pot.
You want to do a job?   Then,
stop fucking yrself.

17

217 Randolph Pl NE
Washington 2 DC
November 20, 1950

My dear Cid Corman:

Now this letter (just read) from you makes
sense, and I thank you for it, thank you for the pressure of feeling
which has made yr words behave.

Fact is, such a letter does what
you think two hours of conversation might (welcome that, tho I may).
For I am a writer.   Which makes me a hearer (or vice-versa) and,
all I have been complaining abt, is, not what you are but what you don't
make yr words say.   Or something.

Do, Cid, stay so nice & simple,
straight: most of the things that we need to say to each other can be
just that.   I have certain things to offer.   You can choose or not to take
them.   All the necessary saying goes in between those two facts.

The
double fact is, you come through, in such a letter as this, are aroused.
Such a sentence as, "Now you are hurting yrself more than me", is
good to hear, sticks, adds something to my day.   And that's something
to be thankful for.

I think my crankiness (and it was no more, at any time) was,
with just one thing: that what you have been saying, takes more saying
than you were giving it.   That is, I put myself into that long letter to
you on a mag-today, spent hours making it, hours I might put into verse
or into, say, an article like the PRO-VERSE thing.   Now I have no reason
to think both the letter, and the PV piece, did not change you, or give you
ideas.   But yr letters back were so scattered, unthought, lumpish, I was
left dry & unhappy.

Take now, e.g., yr reaction to my kick at yr phrase
"along the PROJECTIVE trail."   My lord, man, it delights me that you
planned to make that concept the peg of yr editorial or statement.   You
over-act, in taking it out: all I sd was, such a phrase as trail, was cheap.
And lord, boy, it sure is: a man doesn't put his seriousness out there in
public to be handled jocularly.   But I dare say, in the editorial, you would
not be so careless.   So why be less careful with me?   Fact is, we have
to, one to one, be *more* precise, in a real sense, than in such more
generalized places.

But I think we are squared away at last, and I am glad.   I shall
hope so, for, as I have told you & others, the very existence of such a
magazine as you project, is a happy thing (especially, I keep saying over

to myself, fr BOSTON! (I had occasion to read I, MAX here last week, and it still moves me to the bottom of my feet that, such, is, to be, there, on yr pages, ♯1, for example: it is like an epistle of an apostle fr Rome to the Ephesians when it takes its place in yr pages!) . . .

Well, that for today.   And best luck, as you go along.

19

[217 Randolph Pl   Washington]   Sat nov 25   50

My dear CC:
                    Thank you for yr letters, the 2nd of which came
this a.m.
                    (1) opening, and then not closing a parenthesis, is merely
to acknowledge that just that way is the way one does parenthesize,
actually: true to feeling (don't let the other convention trouble you,
for it's only conventional)

                    (2) like such titles much more, as The
Spring & The Source.   (In fact, if you cared for The Gate & The
Center, I have no objection to yr using that.)   But I like S&S, very
much.

                    (3) spoke to Payne long distance night before last.   But
of course any stuff will have to come slow.   (theirs, I mean).   Also
wrote Kitasono & Hirai (SHIGAKU).

                              Keep me posted

20

my dear cid corman:

black mt character walked in just as i was
settin to write you this morning, so, only now, 5:30, have i read
yr second letter in mails today

and most gratifying: you are on the front
burner, lad, and it is most heartening, comes, in fact, at one of those
needed moments   i thank you, deeply

in fact, i am very excited at your plan, to
"filter", as you say, such quotes as you now have from Vince

point was, i was going to write you today, to
let you know how all additional material now shaped up, that is, what
other poems I figured you should see, for selection, and what other
prose (including some decision on a recasting of GATE & CENTER

for i understood, from yr earlier letter this week, that, the time
had come

what i think is immediately important, is, that, you have
much more of the verse   for what i have to say to anyone, in a letter,
arises, actually, from verse done, doing, or abt to be, done (i should
myself want the proportion to be good, in this respect, of, the verse,
in the issue, to the prose, and i am most happy that you put it, that
"there should be, as I see it now, about 5 or 6 more poems of yours".

The hitch is, that some of it, a couple i think belong, are still under hand.

Likewise, some letters, selections from which you might be interested
in (for other areas there covered), I have asked back, to send you.

now that we are squared away, can you spare me one more
week, or, say ten days? to make up a solid package for you to sit down
with, and, in the light of what you now have, see, from your sitting,
what you would like to have?

the other thing is, to tell you, how moving
it is, to hear, for the *1st time*, a man, making a magazine, say, he is
trying "to organize the issue on the principle that the mag ought to be
read from cover to cover as a single effect"   BOY, does that sound

good, to ears, to, ears!

nor shld you worry, abt fiction: fact is, i'd
just guess, that it is more accurate that way, simply because, today,
now, it is not fiction that, any longer, leads out, the dance   (narrative,
is another matter, and, that quality, in No. 1, is, clearly, already in
hand, in yr composition of it—like you say, "like, a novel" !

(in fact, Creeley's
  work is extremely
  important exactly
  as the push beyond
  the fictive)

(i have, by the way,
tried to set this distinction between
the fictive and the narrative of re-
enactment, in some notes called
OUTSIDE, INSIDE, written as an
introduction to Creeley's stories,
five of them, which may be something
you will be interested in, for issue ♯2;

yes, and another idea, for ♯2, wld be, to prepare for you, as final copy,
a piece on Homer and Melville which I once blocked out—or, for that
matter, the third of the tryptich, a thing on Melville & The King James
Version of the Bible (the other of the three being, of course, the Shake-
speare section, in ISH)

i really wouldn't, if i were you, be concerned
abt this fiction question now *at all*: i think you will come to see that it
is a very beautiful *fact*, that yr mag starts as it is   VERY BEAUTIFUL.
And TELLING.

one other thing: i don't know whether i told you i think yr name
for the mag is definitely on the right track   anyhow, i sat here by the
fire last night trying to put my finger on what did not seem quite right,
why, i was not quite satisfied.   And suddenly I figured it out, and i pass
it on, for what it is worth to you.   My conclusion was, that the trouble
lay, with the /—that the / was artificial or made the thing look self-conscious.
And then i saw it printed, and, figured, maybe, Cid hadn't visualized
how, the/becomes unnecessary, thus:

look—

re SOURCE

or better

re   SOURCE

in other words, that, merely, in the choice of the type, and of the
spacing both horizontally (lead) and vertically (the lower case, upper
case of the font) you can get not only all you want by that separation

of the / but also, by removing it, add to the double entendre

anyhow, there it is, for your pleasure

well, you know i am at work, have been, on the rest of the material.
and shall have it ready any day soon.   but if you are pushed, and
want me to start it coming at you, let me know, and i'll not wait to make
it all a single package

                    let me hear
                              and again, my very fullest
                              thanks

23

cid

'friday   [23   December   50   217 Randolph Pl   Washington]

look: a series of the damndest things, just abt since i wrote
you
            (1)   was setting off for Yucatan today
            (2)   had seven guests fr Black Mt
            (3)   and then, 48 hrs ago, learned my mother was
                  seriously ill

so, making now, for Mass., and hope, somehow, if things are
not too bad, to see you

In any case, I have not forgotten, and will carry along all mss
which are pertinent.

Stand by to hear from me.

                                        Cordially

                        (forgive

24

My dear Cid Corman:

Here it is, entire, the package, I promised you.
(January 12, 1951)

I tell you what: my impression is, this time,
(& the material sitting as it is, as of, now: plus your moxt exciting
plan to weave the letter-passages, as skein) that, the thing to do, is,
to maintain one tone.
(I should imagine that, the work of the others,
will, relieve it!)

So I have selected the package, both the verse,
and the prose.   And, with one exception, I think it does all go together.
Thus, you can select or order or re-order with no anthological
problems!   This is all, all, one face of the character, olson!

(The excep-
tion—what you already have, ISSUE, MOOD.   Which, it is my impression,
let's hold over for some further issue, when, along with it, we can get
in, if you choose, more variety.)

SO: for yr taking: it would be (I summarize, only to be clear, myself):

LES LETTRES (as you have them, and as you want anything
more from me, yes?)

I, MAXIMUS OF GLOUCESTER, TO YOU   (my proud baby)

THE GATE & CENTER   (with what rewrite you shall ask of me)

plus the enclosed:

THE ESCAPED COCK (which seems to me a pair with, THE
G & C and LES LETTRES & which
could, as could THE G & C, be broken
back to form a part of, LES LETTRES ?)

& a verse-prose:

THE STORY OF AN OLSON, AND BAD THING

& the songs:

ADAMO ME

THE MOON IS THE NUMBER 18

It excites me very much, this, this hammering, this, actually, this
axe-head!   O, Corman, that, if it happens, if you like it as a whole,
that, out of Boston, as ORIGIN, this, this should, come!   O, lad, you,
shall have, you, my, such, thanks, such, thank you that you had the
energy, the will, the push to DO IT!

Which squares us away, I think & hope, yes?   Abt the time you get this
we will be picking our way southward, for my first vacation in seven—
count 'em—years.   There will be no new address until I get there.   So,
please, do not let that delay you, or impede you, one bit: write to me
here, and it will follow me as I direct, until I know what our address
will be in Yucatan, which I will send you, almost on arrival.   (I do not
have money enough to stay long, so, for that short time, let's us
communicate by air mail, yes? counting the cost against sun, yes?
(Only a couple of cents more, actually.

And very fast.
Depend upon it.   For your work,
& the future of ORIGIN,
is important

. . . Which does it, yes, as of the moment, except that, to answer yr
letter yesterday—to thank you for it, and to allow, I'll answer other
things, like space, as I go, please?

For we are jumpy with, the getting away, shots, how to leave the
house, what clothes (to press) ((instead of, what ought, to buy)) what
shoes (to have tapped), etc.—so, please, excuse, this latter half
of this letter: I put all my mind into, the 1st, half.

And thanks to you, for the action of, from your heart, yr hand: &
    to yr angel (who sounds so close) best health and, the strength,
      of yr affection

            all love, as I leave

LERMA   CAMPECHE MEXICO   (do *not* put Yucatan: it was my own
                                 error—slows mail one full day)
          Friday Feb 9

My dear Cid:

          Yr letter of last Sat just in, and I make haste to tell
you I have it, and that I am now here, and, for the moment, based &
a little squared away.   I am sorry I have been so slow to catch up again
our mutual doings, but—as I may have warned you—travel upheaves
me no end.   I am still thin from it, up in the air (though this time I
imagine it is the language problems which have me on the hook: I have
yet to have two hours to find out what are the simplest laws of Spanish
construction! things have been happening so steadily)

          The two letters you speak of, should be in my hands
tomorrow, I'd guess (we did not get here until this week, and even
then had a hell of a mess on our hands, this huge house covered with
plaster, every tile.   And we had to take it in that condition or go
without.   So we have had to spend more time here with pails and scrub
brushes, than with head or sun!
                              ((What kept us, longer than just the
boat fr New Orleans to Progreso, was, that, because I was up there
to the northeast, I decided to go to Chichen first.   The which was
something, & right to do, though the almost total loss of the color that
the place wore when it was alive, makes it, so inaccurate that, to a
documentarian like myself, I am as teased out of depth as I am by this
living where the speech is (for me) primitive—rudimentary, rather.

(((But what is alive, and, is the very most exciting thing of all for me,
is Mayan, the language!   And I have already started to learn as much of
it as I can; so much more important to me than Spanish.   In fact, if I
were of dreams, instead of the usual amount of human stupidity, in five
weeks I would constitute myself what they call around here a "Mayista"
(in distinction fr "archeologista").   For already I smell things in these
living Maya which are gates to now & then more solid than stones.
                                                        In this
connection, within two hours of arrival in Merida, I had learned of two
powerful things of Barlow (whom you will recall I promised to enlist
for ORIGIN):
               (1) a yr ago, unknown to me, he had done precisely
                    what I have now done (and, of course, with supreme
                    equipment, he)—had settled at Telchac (another
                    fishing village like this one, on the north coast of
                    the peninsula, near Progreso) to master this speech,
                    in order, I should imagine from my own temper, to
                    go in by way of it to those passages of man that
                    archeologists do not get to
                                    ((it is wild, the way all

the big guns of Carnegie &
Peabody etc., actually rest
their careers on a people whose
whole value, recovered, is aesthetic,
and yet, with the possible exception
of Tozzer (& among the young Barlow)
they themselves are without aesthetic
comprehension!))

In other words, Barlow was taking the step which the present demands of
any worker anywhere: SOUNDS.

(2).   The second fact of Barlow is as
tragic a thing as I have known now for sometime: one month ago, in his
house in the suburb of Mexico City called Atzcapotzalco, he dismissed
his boys (he lived alone, was, c 35) wrote them a letter in Mayan, and
killed himself with an overdose of sleeping pills.   You will gather, from
the way I used him as a point d'appui to you, how very much of a loss I
think this is to all contemporary America.   ((His reasons, so far as I
have been able to talk to those who knew him in Telchac and in Merida,
are wholly obscure.

It is unbearable, that he is lost, right now, for
the work that needs to be done.   I am heart-broken I shall not have the
chance I so deeply looked forward to, to meet him, here, or in Mexico
City this year. . . .

I cannot think of a man who was so clearly that
combination I would see as just as much prime to creative work now
as the androgyne is to politics (Mao, say), the former combination
that of documentarian & the selectivity of the creative taste & mind.

. . . Do say hello to Vinc & Peg for me, and tell them I shall be writing to
them as soon as I can find out such things as where one gets milk, how
to say basin in the market, and to manage to make our Indian landlord
get a plumber to flush the toilet!   (We are that close to beginning life—
even on the skirts of such a civilization as the Maya!)

my dear Cid:

        A note, quickly, to thank you for your letter, which just
came, and to tell you that the rewrite of G & C is under hand (yr other
letter, about it, to Washington, arrived here yesterday; on my own part
I wish to lighten some of the emphasis on Waddell's book, to keep the
whole piece from being squeezed into too narrow a reference.   For it is
not Waddell, but the refreshment of values so far as history goes, that
I am after.   As the final version came out, it bore down a little too
specifically on arguable historical event (such as the King-Lists).   But
it is minor change.   And should free the whole into a lighter air.   I
shall also try to avoid lambasting those ex-confreres, the modern
academics, like you say.

        One thing, though: it means very much to me that you
should lead me off, in issue #1, with a poem, not with G & C.   My impression
is, that yr original intention, was to use I, MAX, as the first of my things,
yes?   I should be very much obliged if you will still do that, in fact,
precisely because it is an epistle, and a sort of opener of the can, as
well as a poem, it does do what I think you yrself are after: no matter
what prose is, it is not, if it is not a story, a created thing as is a
poem.
        ((It is even, is it not, a sort of bowsprit, with figurehead, no?
        that thing I am so soft abt, I, MAXIMUS OF GLOUCESTER, TO YOU

. . . I'm afraid I don't know enough to visualize photo-offset, but, so far as
smoking out further funds, I think the handsomer and solider you make
issue #1 the more you are likely to harvest (Americans being so easily
impressed by appearance).   You will, of course, know best.   Tell me,
what is the type-face such offset allows?

You know, there *is* one help you could give me on this Maya thing.   I
cannot buy or even borrow, here in Yucatan or Mexico, a copy of Alfred
Tozzer's A MAYA GRAMMAR WITH BIBLIOGRAPHY AND APPRAISE-
MENT OF THE WORKS NOTED, Papers, Peabody Museum of American
Archeology and Ethnology, Harvard University, Vol. 9, 1921.
        I wld write
to Peabody direct, but the trouble is, for the book to be of any use to me,
I ought to have it long before I am told it would reach me, parcel post.
Obviously air mail would be the answer, but I have no way of knowing
how heavy Vol 9 of such studies is, and dasn't commit myself to the cost,
without knowing.   (The book itself, I am told, is only $3.50).
        Could you,
without spending too much time, determine how best to handle this?   It
would be a great help.   And if it works out that it can be solved without
much trouble & without too much in addition to the cost of the book (maybe

air parcel post?), and you could manage the dough, I can reimburse
you by check (the advantage, to me, if you could do it, without further
consultation, is, of course, time). . .

It was damn nice of you to think of offering to aid me on any such stuff.
And curious, that, this very day, I had been asking myself, how can I
get the Tozzer! So you musn't feel jumped. It was, stars! Echoes!!

In any case, Peabody Museum ought to know all the answers on mailing,
they being in such touch precisely with Yucatan: it just might happen
they are flying down a man, or something, this week, who might carry
same to Merida, and mail to me, say, if he were traveling light.

Well, I toss it to you, and shall be mucho gratias, for whatever, you
find possible.

. . . Write as much and as soon as you can. Will see that G&C gets off
to you, despite the terrible temptations: to swim, to go into the hills
and hunt ruins, or just to loll!

30

cid:
     yr letter just in, and i have an idea—

1st, i think (though I certainly grant the necessities of cost any man
printing today faces) that you ought to take further steps to exhaust
the possibility of type before you go into that modern monster, varitype.
For this battle too is a part of the battle of culture now (in fact, that
ugly thing, modern economy, is precisely squeezing you when it pushes
you away from type to a machine which, was invented is advertized and
exists only by the inexcusable uses it offers to BUSINESS)

on top of that, as i sd to you earlier this week, i am very much afraid
(going by my own taste as somewhat   a measure   of the kind of people
to whom you must look for support once the magazine is started) that
you will, with varitype, be penny wise

but i want to offer you more than merely the objections of my taste,
as well as predictions.   i want to offer you help in cutting through this
damnable barrier modern economy has put us all in:

(1)   my thinking went this way, that, somewhere in the environs of
      Boston, there *must* be a printer with some of the old feel plus
      an economic situation which does not involve big city costs

      my mind went to Cummington, of course, thinking that it just
      might be that that gang up there (who are, of course, like all
      literary printers, somewhat too fancy for my taste) anyhow, that
      that gang up there might just be looking for a chance to put in
      to a magazine like yrs (now you may well not want any such extra
      engagement of persons, but, at least, I don't imagine such would
      interfere with you as Brandeis proposed)

      in any case, I rather think you would be happier with a job printer:
      have you asked, and asked, abt such, in any small town near you?
      any man who is good and yet who hungers for a chance to do more
      than letter-heads?

BUT (2), then, on the pot, I got hot: look   LOOK   sitting right out there
      in Hyde Park, suddenly I realized, are two of the best birds I knew
      at Black Mountain (where almost all such are trained to presswork),
      Paul Williams and Dan Rice, plus a lad named, I think, John
      Dickinson, who writes with considerable distinction (I noticed him
      first, along with Perchik, in "Resistance")

NOW I am writing after this note to you, to Williams and Rice, asking
them if they are there, and to get in touch with you if they have any
ideas to offer (Williams is as highly trained a man in modern
processes and machines as I know, and you can depend absolutely
on him: as well, he is sweet to the core, tough worker, and gifted

on top of that, both Williams and Rice are close to me, and would
if there is any chink in the wall, put their hearts in to getting
out a handsome issue ♯1 of ORIGIN

PLEASE   do not Commit yrself to varitype until these
—————   friends have had a chance, at least, to *help!*
———
—

                      Love & quick

lerma   march 1, 51
campeche

my dear cid:

            i hope you'll agree, it came out wonnerful!   i am very
pleased it shrank (as you thot it might, too), for it now carries its weight
(Waddell) much more lightly, much less by argument, much more by
tale & assertion.   And I am extremely pleased Part 1 is back to the sort
of clog & shuffle it was in the 1st place, a sort of turkey trot, before,
the laying of, the egg!   (Part II, the EGG!)   In any case, it is what I
was after, and I send it off to you, air mail, complete copy, with a
certain sense of immense satisfaction (I never, as you knew, liked the
version you had: it got too much Waddell and thus obscured, the real
point, of, where we are, and how we go ahead.)

            at the same time, i have, i hope, obviated all the difficult-
ies of profanity as off-beat anger which you wrote to me about: i think the
only suggestion you made which i have not followed exactly, is, to remove
Soc from the opening para.   But, as you see, I have removed the nasty word.
((Please go along with me, in leaving him there, right at the start, even
    tho I can see yr point, that, he may seem to make a stumble for the rea-
    der.   (But if the style is going to be entered on anyway, by any alive
    reader, he can't say I didn't forewarn him!)   No.   But seriously, I want
to assure you, that, in hanging one on Soc, I am being accurate: he is
as much a Sacred Cow to be slaughtered, cut up, disposed of, as is
his Twin, CHRIST.   And he stands, and should stand, right there, off
the bat, as THE ENEMY.   For he is (I have not, for so many years,
been engaged in dialectic, for nothing: if you watch, you will discover
that, in conversation after c., you are shadow-boxing that old bastard,
that old divinely gifted but false man—he is much more the BIG GUY
than Plato, much more the significant force (Plato was just a tremendously
gifted re-write man, of same Soc)
                                ((it would be a telling thing, if
someone would do a book, entitled SOCRATES AND CHRIST, and—
doing exactly opposite of Dahlberg—see them not as heroes but as devils))

But my big pleasure is, that the piece is now in a compass exactly right
for its tone.   The which is the job I owed you.   Take it, with my thanks,
that you are giving it print. . . .

I hope by now Paul Williams and you have got together, that, between you
you may have, somehow, obviated vari-type.   In any case, please write me
back about everything, how all goes, and what's the schedule ahead: you
will imagine that, as the DAY comes closer, I am beginning to heat up,
from anticipation!
                        All best, all ways

[on front of envelope]

"o my sone, rise from thy bed. . .

        work what is wise"

34

el
CID:

monday morn, march 6, arrived (1) TOZZER, grammar & (2) MAP, area, fr Tulane, so, am squared away, and, most importantly, on lengua, thanks to you: I enclose check for DOLLARS 4.39, but with this injunction: it is the very last money I have in bank (that is, my uncertain bookkeeping shows, 6 bucks, even, meaning, the 4.39 ought not to bounce, and if you are severly pressed, you might take a chance. However, if you can wait until my bank balance comes thru fr Washington (it usually comes there the 25th of the month), I can make you absolutely certain (and save myself a buck charge, for their lousy services on a bounced check: you see, the only reason I am slightly nervous, is, that, I never know what charges they are adding anyhow, for their miserable little check charges, etc., even when the money they are using for their usury is mine, solid, good earned money, for goods exchanged—my goods, obviously, being, when any money is earned, not the product of my labor but, the natural resources herein contained.   The more I think of it, the more strongly I hope you can hold it for a few days, until I can let you know it's good dough—o, wait a minute, I know how to solve this: let me send you the stamp value in stamps! And the book value by check. Then you will have what you put out, and also, there shld be left, in my account, enough to cover any of those damnable charges of theirs for using *my* money:

        ((I find myself so often agreeing with
        EZ's economics, when it is this ele-
        mentary, that is, that, what was lost
        (by the increase of population—this is
        not EZ's insight, alas, and thus, his
        whole argument is deeply invalidated—
        HONESTY, as a prime of behaviour in
        a town or a city) ((around these parts,
        e.g., a while back, if a man was a
        thief, he was, discovered, from then on,
        the slave of the man he stole from, for
        life!))

        with honesty gone, it was no longer
        possible for money to stay where it
        belongs, in a man's jeans

        Or, otherwise, a bank shld pay me for
        keeping (using) the money, instead of
        the reverse.))

And delighted, that you got together with BMC three: two, rather, plus Dickinson, whom I hoped, out of it, you wld like the prose of: he is a sort of antique American thing, the blueberry time, simpliccimus, Thoreau-time, the positionalism (& nerves) BEFORE quantity—the above, plus natural resource, due to machine—became the contradictory, but leading principle of modern life:

I am getting so sick of the inability of our freres to come to grips with the change that the tripling of world population (& the what-ing of world resources) in the past 100 years (or 150?) has done to values, that I am tempted right this day to sit down and write out for you (for a later ORIGIN) exactly how this change has effected ALL (equals everything)

But it still seems to me so obvious & so prime, that, the dopes, they should not need to be drilled (Ortega put it out on the table for them some certain years ago) ((tho with a twist which is pedantic of him, existenz, even tho Spanish—Unamuno was a truer man))

So please write again soon.   And I will.   This, to thank you MUCHO MUCHO

[Lerma]   Monday March 12, 1951

My dear Cid:

        . . . I am spent, today: gave a lot of time, last week, to
the field.   It is a pleasure, as you'd guess, but damned difficult on
the system, and yesterday and today, I have had to lie low.   The dust,
when you are pulling out the face of a ruin, for fragments, is
terribly fine, and clogs my chest rapidly, giving me almost a form
of pneumonia.   Yet I can't stay away!   And walking, now, in the
sun, any time after 10, at the latest, in the morning, is murder:
it is not possible to move again until 4 in the afternoon.
                                        But I made
progress, by that kill, last week.   Have the problem now in shape.
And it is big: it comes out thus—THE SEA, in MAYAN ECONOMY,
and ITS EFFECTS on THEIR CULTURE AND ART.   What I need, now,
is

(1)   moneys, fr some foundation, to keep me in the field, here

(2)   a jeep

(3)   a schooner, or launch, to survey the sites of the whole
       coast, the East side as well as, now that I have sketched
       it, this West north and south of me here (for example, the
       greatest sea site of all, yet known, is the Isla de Jaina,
       just north of us about 20 miles.   And cannot be got to
       except fr sea.)

(4)   books, or, in lieu of that, airplane money to shoot to
       Merida & back

So you see how impossible it all is!

                In a sense, it doesn't matter.   There is much I can
turn my hand to, I suppose this disappointment (for I don't see how
yet to make a push for such a stake, even, for the smallest part of
it, just the small moneys to go on living here, and traveling, the
hard way) is of little moment.   For example, yesterday, lying low,
if I didn't start a piece on Dahlberg's last book!   Maybe, if I keep
interested, it might be something you would be interested in, for a
future number: it would have to be a study of demonism in the present
society.   And, perhaps, by it, I could take the step further that you
suggest, on SOC & CHRISTOS: for Dahlberg is profoundly wrong
(which is a great way to be, if you can't be profoundly right—a proposition, by the way, that would need proving to our lazy time, despite
their secret acknowledgements of such demons as Hitler, say).   And
both Soc and Christ are figures he works his wrongs out by way of:
(if you have the Roditi piece you mentioned on Dahlberg handy, shoot

it to me, if you can: I'd be curious, to see his argument against D)

    Well, this is just to thank you, and to tell you I am alive and at
it.   Do write.

O, yes: is it going to be possible
for you to send me proofs? I hate
both to ask it and to do it, but,
my experience is, printers never
believe the spaces I leave are
serious. And fuck up any no. of
effects, thereby.
                  Do let me have yr best thought, on this.

Another idea, for future no.: thru
Gus Stromsvik, the Carnegie's tough field boss,
I have come to know and enjoy one Hippolito Sanchez, in
the Campeche Museum (he comes for dinner tonight).

What's important, are his drawings of the glyphs at
Copan: they are the finest things since Catherwood's,
my impression is, finer. Now I don't know how you are
going to be set up for repros, ahead. But keep in mind
that, if any such thing becomes possible, no more
beautiful and interesting presentation of the force of
this language-design which is called Maya can be gotten
than Sanchez's *unpublished* drawings.

lerma, campeche, mex
march 22? anyway Bad
friday

cid:

       mucho trabajo (which gets sd, again & again, hereabouts):
3 hrs & 1/2 yesterday tearing down the side of a cut in a cuyo (man
ruin) near here—much dust, but many things, excellent pot frags, &
a fine stucco ear tabret, as well as curious round pieces with holes in
them, used, I figure, as decorative raises on headdress (this particular
ruin is a little jewel.   And today the owner comes, to see what arrange-
ment we can make for taking it apart—one trouble is, americans, previously, have wanted whole figures, & jade pieces, which I don't give
a damn abt.   But, that they did, makes natives think, I am digging
for same.   Which hampers.)

       mucho gracias, for yr letter, all abt, business of, ORIGIN—
(by the by, you will imagine how delightful the name comes across,
down here, with one's hands in, just such, as of, the peopling of,
this continent: if i can establish it, i may have for you a piece, one day,
connecting up, this demonstration to, proposals of, G & C!)

       ...i was delighted with yr Albanian, and if you keep in touch
with him, let me know, for, whenever i have in hand proof on PRAISES,
& can release a copy of IN COLD HELL, IN THICKET, i should like to
send it to him, for a present, just to show him (probably lover of Hafiz),
how much ceremony there is, now!   for he deserves it, for using the
word, ceremony, beautiful concept that it is!   (He sounds like one of
those wonderful resistant men that migration still leaves gaping, like
lovely fish, on that ugly shore, the united states of america)....

       you haven't sd anything abt proofs—and it begins to get close
to April 15.   Is it hopeless?   If so, please, go over all olson with someone,
will you?   that is, watch carefully for (1) the spacing, that, it keep the
same proportions I get fr this machine (print or varitype space is different,
and it is the feeling of the equivalent proportion that i am after)

& (2)—what is always a trouble—that, my line is often so long, it
overhangs, in type, and so, I have always the headache that, tradition
calls for the overhung line to go all the way back to the left margin,
when, for my effects such is disastrous: it should, any overhung line,
be placed at the *right* margin, the end of the word or phrase coinciding
with the end of the line which it is organically a part ((I think you have
a copy of Montevallo R, with Kingfishers: it is not still all right, but,
I did the proofing as best I can, and you will see, there, how I want an
overhung line to work))

O, yes, (3) indentations, that is, the *other* spacing problem, the space
           I intend fr left to right: this is always being tampered with,
           by printers—please, here, too, see, that the relative
           proportions are accomplished, yes?

I shall be most grateful to you, if you can't send proofs, if you will be
this kind, and take the time I know it, hopingly, takes, to do this for me.
For—as you yrself—I know I have a damn irritating style of punctuation
& placements (I do it gravely, as a part of, my method, believing that,
resistance must be a part of style if, it is a part of the feeling)—and
if errors creep in, palpable errors, then, the whole careful structure
comes down.   For then any fresh or new placement or punctuation,
instead of creating eventual confidence in the reader, seems, instead,
to be a cause for uneasinesses
                              And it is the more necessary in varitype,
simply because (1) varitype is relatively new, and the reader not yet
accustomed to its face,

        &(2), the major problem of it, for my money, that, varitype,
for some reason of the engineering of its machine, allows altogether
too much space to the thin letters, conspicuously "i" and "l", thus creating,
where there are combinations of same, a tremendous hole in the word,
and, generally, gives a loose & porous look to the page
                                            (this difficulty is
obviated, by the way, in *italic* varitype, due to the slanting & hooks-like-
handwriting, joining the letters together & giving a much more continuous,
& flowing, effect: I'd call yr attention to this font, for future issues, if
you haven't already used it)

I am frankly scared to death of this "i", "l" problem.   Tho I don't see
how you can avoid it except by using the italic font.   In any case, that
openness, looseness, does, for me, make it imperative that all other
spaces be exact.

I mention this all to you, not to carp, Cid, not to admit yr problems,
but to ask you to give me this extra attention, simply because I fear
you will not be able to send me proofs.   And I think you would want my
text to be as exact, in its effects, as I would.

((I also, by the way, just to register it with you, for what it is worth,
   think that the smaller point type faces in varitype are preferable—
   for one thing they clear the face of its too close resemblance to type-
   writer face (thus, mimeograph); and also, because I don't think
   varitype has the range of hand or machine-set type face, declare, for
   varitype, a sort of convention it badly needs: it looks much cleaner,
   tighter when the point is 6 or 7, on the outside 8))

God knows you got problems.   And I know that.   I say these things,
because, talking abt proof, they come up into my mind.   So take them,
please, in that spirit.
                ((((And excuse me a little, for, as I don't think
you would know, graphics was, once, a little bit my profession: Ben
Shahn and I were, once, a "team"!))))

. . . . Anyway, I await all, eagerly: please keep writing

my dear cid Corman—surely, you deserved instant reply, for yr excellent
idea, that we double the push of the glyph-drawings by yr adding a show in
some Boston museum, is wonderful
                              & i went at it, to answer you, instantly: the only
trouble was, it was Holy Sat, & when i got in to the museum, no one, no
one!   On Monday, Pavon, the director, was gone, flown to Mexico City
for conferences.   So, the final decision (which, fr Sanchez' position, has
to be Pavon's) must wait until the first of next week.
                                        HOWEVER: it has
been very fortunate.   For all this week, each day, I have gone in to the
museum, & Sanchez and I are in the process of going over each of the
full page drawings of the Copan glyphs, so that I am completely familiar
with what there is.   And, by the end of the week, I should be ready to
select what, & all, drawings which you can use (1) for the magazine and
(2) for a gallery show. . . .

Please let me know as soon as you can how far you are able to take this
thing.   And I will let you know instantly that we have Pavon's decision
(I can't see how he can refuse to let Sanchez use *some* of his drawings
 for ORIGIN, but how far further he will go I can't say; I have a few
tricks up my sleeve to pull him by—for he is an ambitious man—and
I ought to be able to pull him all the way over.   But he is a scholar,
and you know how scholars are, about "ART"—they are not timid, but
they are careful, that what is their baby isn't allowed to get over to the
people.   For they know that that masonism of their profession is what
keeps them at posts, & insures them that security of job & reputation
which, always, in the end, kills them off!
                              But there is one other useful
thing I know about him, beside the fact that he can supply, for the show,
exact readings of all glyphs (Pavon is the best of the contemporary Mexican
specialists in the glyphs as calendars: J. Eric Thompson, the big gun
(Carnegie), in his last book, 1950, speaks of Pavon as "a star on the
horizon"!   Pavon is young, and sharp.   And the other thing, which he has
to offer, is excellent photographs of the stones in situ, excellent ones,
which could be (some blown up, perhaps) interspersed with the drawings
as a constant reminder to the looker-on that, it is STONE, that is being
demonstrated, as an ART . . .
                              JESUS.   The more it unfolds under hand,
the more I think you have the hottest of hot ideas for an auxiliary drama-
tization of ORIGIN's force in contemporary culture: and to dramatize it
by way of GLYPHS, fr the oldest and purest *origin* on this continent, this
hemisphere!   WOW. . . .

God, but it's HOT: and i shall be delighted, if anyone wants it, to write
my first go at THE ART OF THE LANGUAGE OF MAYAN GLYPHS, for
a catalogue, or whatever, you can damn well bet a cocoa bean (good

Mayan money) on that!   As well as I think I can get Pavon to do a
fresh take on the glyphs as time celebrants

I'm telling you, Cid, you have in yr hands the makings of one of those
shows (like the Armory Show, 1913, wasn't it, which blew the States
across, with the French) or, more to my wonder, that show the Mus
of Mod Art, in NY, shot over, years ago, on the ART OF THE CAVES
(organized, by god, by Leo Frobenius—which fact is so little remem-
bered I have never seen anyone point it out)...

Well, with Pavon's okay, we're launched.   I hope you will like these
extensions of your own suggestion, for which I, and Sanchez, are
immensely grateful.

WE'LL BANG 'EM!

...—and you understand, of course, that this job that Pavon and Sanchez
did, on the spot, at Copan, is the FIRST TIME that all the glyphs at one
place have been RECORDED—and there were important discoveries,
one of which would bring every maya expert in the place to see the show:
on STELA I (eye), due to Sanchez's drawing, Pavon discovered an
eclipse of the sun which the Washington Observatory confirmed the
date of, which confirmation in its turn confirms the absolute correctness
of the Goodman-Martinez-Thompson correlation formula for relating
Maya dates to Christian calendars (and was, and, with this show, shall
be, great NEWS)

O, lad, you have a golden egg, yes, a gold & egg, eck, shoosh, ek!

lerma   april 8

cid:
          thank you for yr good letter, abt all things
                                              and do excuse me, i
waited until i had Pavon's final word on whether, right now, he could
allow Sanchez (1) to give us drawings for ORIGIN, & (2) for a show.
                                                                And
the son-of-a-bitch!   He says, NO!   I am so gd sore I can't see, and poor
Sanchez: he's as gloomy as possible for man to be.   And rightly so.   For,
there is no reason why, despite the contract (so far as the Copan stuff
goes) with the Honduran Govt, there is no earthly reason why Pavon
shouldn't do the customary thing, ask permission of them for Sanchez
to use what selection you might want, at least, for the mag...

In any case, do keep open, as long as you can, your wonderful idea of
a Mayan issue: let me turn that one over a bit, and see what I can raise
up—it might also be an excellent one in which to frame Barlow's work, eh?

Things are a little tightened, as the money begins to squeeze, and so
time gets me by the short hairs.   But still turn up enough, at the moment,
to keep running myself over like I was a Mack truck.   Will write more on
this.

For now the big thing is ORIGIN, and has me, too, holding, waiting!   Do
send me the earliest possible copy you can, by air....

                                 i   Well, lad, this
to catch you in the last hours!   And to wish it godspeed.   Please write
me all back, as fast, as you have news, eh?   Most jumpy!

43

cid corman   cid corman
LAD   cid corman   CID
cid corman   cid corman

lerma   FRIDAY MORNING
April 27   1951

the fullest satisfaction i have ever had from print, lad, the fullest.
And i am so damned moved by yr push, pertinence, accuracy, taste,
that it is wholly inadequate to say thanks.

it's the sort of satisfaction i suppose a man damn well rarely has

(i should make immediately clear, that i don't mean as of my own
 stuff at all, or that i am featured, both of which make me squirm,
 that, *all* is not at all, not anywhere near, good enough, *not* at all

but that so long as it is, you have given it the very maximum chance—
and that, by god, is something damned unusual, and i am deeply, deeply
pleased

... and the varitype is, actually (i do believe), *better* (in the sense of
the *speed* of it, is damned wonderful: i don't know, others would better
say, but my own impression is, that, the speed of it is damned good
for my kind of language, no?   seems so, the 1st go.   seems exactly
right.   And I agree, the spacing, is ok ok (in fact, doesn't the note
to vinc -42- look just as good as anything ever did?)

I regret one thing, that, MAX, comes off straight fr, instead of fr a
white page, the "introductions" (tho i don't think that's the reason i
don't like the poem at all, this morning: crazy, isn't it, that, the poem
i wanted so hard, 1st, and out there, seems, now that i see it, altogether
bad, altogether sliding, slippery, wrong: somehow, the fish, got out of
his element, and is just slimy, to the touch, on, land.   Definitely have
a horror of it this morning!   (And i keep using the note to vinc -42- as
offset, as, as it is to me, this morning, brandnew, and, very beautiful:
the last four lines are worth all, the MAX)

I know the reasons why you probably felt such introductions were necessary,
(that is, I like very much the whole concept of not having names inside
the mag, yet, at the same time, not making it as foolish (the anonymity)
as those ridiculous TIGER'S EYE people did, like, some sealed envelope
in some contest) i like yr notion of, putting the contents, straight, there,
right off the bat (also yr ordering same, not by alphabet but, by yr own
choice of weights to be emphasized—that's something I think you should
damn well keep (makes for a very nice unsaid direction by, you, the
man whose magazine this is: think, here, you show exactly the same
qualities, the same clean, fine acts, that yr subscription note is the
dignity of

        KEEP ALL THAT, but (1) give the 1st piece in any issue an

open page ahead of itself: not necessarily a whole white page, in fact,
on the contrary, i think not: but give it some breath, the reader, to,
start anew with, the material, after, the intros

                                    & (2), for my taste
(and here is where I say, i understand the reason, that is, the
"humanization" of, the individuals, but, one thing i wld do another
   time is, be quite formal abt, whoever it is, whose work you are,
   listing: that is, yr own prose in the subscriber note is impeccable,
    shows, you deeply are, formal—and I think the introductions call for
just that same quality, in the statement of, whatever it is you want

(AND I ABSOLUTELY GO FOR YOUR USING THE WHOLE INTRO AS
   YOU HAVE USED IT—to fold away what you think is, the importances)

to put, there, abt, any of sd persons, or, the mag

You see, Cid, what this mag establishes, beyond a doubt, is, that you
are a man of courtesies.   Which is precious.   And is a quality beyond
compare.   (You handle everyone, in the intro, including the thank you,
with a delicate and exact courtesy.   So you need have no doubts, what-
so-ever.   You can be quite full of confidence, in, yr notes.   You come
across very very nicely.   (I mean, example, the "plus some notes of
my own that inadvertently got into the text"—nice, the way, that,
inadvertently, poses, itself!)

(O, ya: an idea—if you are going to keep the epigraph, i have a
   suggestion, to push it, to make it work, harder—and to take off
   any curse of "wisdom saying": that is, drop it, thus:

          "O my son, arise from thy bed---work
             what is
             wise"

Jesus, tho, how, the whole thing is, IS.   How it sets itself out there,
straight.   Direct.   No crap.   Nice.   Itself.   (And that's your doing,
absolutely: it is a proud biz, and you have the right of, pride.   I am
so very very damned glad abt it, damned, GLAD.

That is (as above, the intros, others (peter russell, say) *have* to
put their personalities out, you don't, yours, is already there, sharp,
clear, in the whole thing—deeply imbedded in every damn bit of the
whole piece—the whole, mag.   It is very wonderful, damned much
object (thus, disclosure, without, statements).   This is what makes
me so very excited abt you, abt, ORIGIN 1, as, here, it is, in my hand!

(And, by the way, tho, I suppose, it came natural, like they say, yet,
   the use of italics, for the letters, giving that difference, is, very

damned good, too

> And, so far as i have now read, the choice, of
> type face variants within, the mag, seem to me
> to be allright (let me, later, when i have read it
> all, say, on this, eh?).   But the 1st impression
> is, the change of pace is, very proper. . . .
>
> Or are the variations simply, the em quads, &
> sizes, not, face variants?   I guess that's it, fr
> a quick study, eh?   Anyway, it's nice; and the
> inking, by, whoever, is damned good, too: is
> very even throughout which must, no?, be a
> sort of triumph with, varitype, no?

One other demur: (and i think it hinges on, too many different type
variants on *one* surface, and a small, immediate one at that) is,
the COVER.

> Here, again, basically, it's fine, very, fine.   But

(1)   I'd give the dark o r i g i n more space to itself

&   (2)   drop the masking on the border—which, to my eye, introduces a
distraction—that is, such a simple straight space, presenting
itself in one glance, gains (again) by, severity & formality:

(the bold 1 looks handsome, i think

You are aware, I'm sure, of how thoroughly right the thing is, to have,
as it has (the whole mag) a density *inside*: the size of the page, plus
the way the thing (without interruption of names) goes right abt its
business, with, the pages nice & thick (fr the small type used).   That's
very damned splendid, and rare, and makes, already, ORIGIN, a stand-out.

Well, christ.   It's a pleasure to write this to you.   And there is nothing
held back, lad.   I've sd it all.   All that I have to say.   So you see how
thoroughly you have done yr job.   Damned wonderful it is.

. . . I dare say everyone will howl at you that there's just too goddamned much
olson (poor lad!).   (I'm not sure I wouldn't myself, given that, he, to me,
here, is all, or too much of, one, say, tone, poor lad!   BUT, fuck em.
For, it is RIGHT, what you are doing, RIGHT, to build by a man, instead
of by, (as per usual),   ABSTRACTIONS—

> one new thing to comfort you, and, to
> give em back, in their face, is, that
> Tatiana Prouskouriakoff, in,
> CLASSIC MAYAN ART (Carnegie, just,
> recently)
> emphasizes, that, every example of

inscription on sculpture in all, all the
whole Mayan area, IS BUILT AROUND—
where there is a figure at all—is built
around, the whole business, the writing
of the glyphs, the presentation of an
offering, anything the inscription sets
out to do:

ONE central HUMAN figure!

(no god, or abstract concept, no "ideas",
  but
        ONE MAN!

so, fr the good past, CON
FIRMATION!

––––––––

I have just this minute read THE STORY OF, and take back what i sd, that
anyone shld object that, there is, too much of, sd, creature.   NOT AT ALL,
god damn it.   For, ADAMO ME, and this STORY, stand up god damn RIGHT!
I am most excited to see them in print.   For, they are, there, what, I
damn well intended.   And are, very much, what I want.   That is, those
two look, proud, are, what they are, definitely, hitting, the two things,
the two, control points, the, job.
                     By god, Cid, that you put those two
in print is ENUF!   Right there is, enough.   right there.   I am damn
well very beautifully pleased with that, alone, those two, YES.

And don't think it didn't take me this one of a hell long time to get to
the point to say this.   And how important it is.   So, that you made it
possible, by, going along to them with, yr taste, and, by yr taste plus
the drive to make the taste out there, you, have given me this
DISCOVERY
            Which is (for my money) proof that, 75 cents, is, exactly
the right price!
                    LOVE,

                            o

                        whom the sun & dust eats

47

cid!

    well, the wildness of it, is not gone, but, i can be, cooler, eh?
that is, all that i sd last week abt the job you've done holds, firm,
firmer in fact— . . .

               take it this way: this mag is yrs.   you are the
governance of each issue just as surely as each man or woman in
same is the governance of any poem or story by that man or woman
in it.   and—what is perhaps the best way to get this across, each issue
of yr mag is, exactly, as a book is: with this tremendous difference,
that, any book is, fr start etc., clearly, all, the governance of the man
who makes all the material in it

    the special problem of an editor is, that, tho he is the governance,
the pieces, he is composing, are, someone else's (chiefly), in other
words that he is the agent of a, collective, right?

    the result usually is, of course, that a magazine becomes an
exercise of taste, that is, that it is the editor's *taste* which is that
quality of his which dominates the governance
                           and (the tough one),
because a literary magazine is, literary, inevitably it is his literary
taste which, leads on, the, whole effect, eh?

Now.   the damnable thing abt this is, that, almost all writers are *also*
essentially agents of, their, literary taste—that is, each poem or
story tends toward a professionalism, tends to seem completed by,
the expression of, that part of, taste!
                    In other words one comes to a
fearful compounding: the character of the work that comes to the hand
of an editor is, chiefly, such, bits of, taste, and he in turn, by what
you might call the compulsions of the vehicle of a magazine of the
"creative", is led on to compose, principally, by a like principle of,
taste, eh?

Now i take it there are only two ways out of this dilemma.   I don't, of
course, go for it, yet, I think any of us ought to admit that, what NINE
is—or was, in its beginning—was a deliberate (& most english, urbane
decision, that, culture (not art, notice) is taste, and that, by the king's
grace, the way to make a magazine is to be wholly professional abt,
taste (and that taste is precisely the inherited mold: why, for example,
there is so much of the Latin poets, in same, Rome being, exactly,
the predecessor of, London as center of the new mercantilism (I am
referring to Elizabethan London, which, was the projector of, what we

call British culture—of which same culture NINE is as precise a new assertion of as is Winston Churchill of feudal politics

What I am urging on you is, a wholly different principle of, governance: simply, that, any given issue of ORIGIN, is, not a *champ clos* (!) of taste alone (which rests—inevitably—on an assumption that the culture system is clear, its validities certain, and its values to be depended on: a closed system)
                that any given issue of ORIGIN will have maximum force as it is conceived by its editor as a FIELD OF FORCE

which brings us to the mat: in what way *can* a magazine for the "creative" be at once the inevitable act of the taste of the editor and at the same time be, wholly, inside itself, a, field of force?

i, frankly, don't know: that is, i take it ORIGIN is about the business of trying to prove exactly that point—how it can be, more than, a collection of, tastes, governed by, the taste of, cid corman, eh?

but what we do know, already, is:
                ONE, that corman is ready to make a mag which reads fr cover to cover (as you put it, so well, yrself, last fall) like a book, eh?   that is, that, already, you are going on a premise other than, taste
        ((this has to follow, if i am right, that, a mag is not
         a book, in that, it is not all one man's material

        ORIGIN is not also an anthology

        and O is not also, a magazine with some, extra-
        literary purpose, that is, is not like so many of
        those political hybrids of the 30's (Partisan R, as
        the last, to stick around). Or one of the newest fads,
        like, say, NEUROTICA—psychiatry, e.g., being one
        of those latest diversions of, the body, politick, which
        introduce false leaders into, this problem of, a
        "creative" magazine

TWO: O is "*for* the creative", that is, as yr subscriber note so finely had it, "present & future, our most active participation" and "that the best of it builds fr, our, arts"—in other words, that, O, is OPEN (is not at all assuming that culture (which is not art alone) is set

Which (the way i keep recurring to, this opposition of—in the mind behind O, or, any mag today solving the problem other than say, NINE's way—

this opposition of art & culture) seems to me to offer us the clue, that is

THAT ORIGIN PRESENTS THE SAME PROBLEM AS—I take it—A POEM OR STORY DOES, now:

> that, because it is OPEN, & it already implies that ENERGY is the source of, taste (which seems to be the way a man of art would see the relation of art to culture in contrast to the man of culture who sees art as spectator, and so, enjoys by way of, essentially, taste (his), alone) by the fact that you have shown already that you are willing to risk an issue of yr magazine on ONE MAN or ONE CONCEPT—a daring thing, that, a mag like NINE, or anyone of 'em, would only do if, they rested on a man whom the taste or culture generally had taken to its bosom (an EZ no., say, or, a WCW, which is, finally, whatever its value, easy)
>> because of these two guide wires, already in there, in the structure—the given—of ORIGIN

> > that THE DEMAND
ON YOU, CID CORMAN, is, to accomplish each issue—to see it, always, clearly, exhaustively, as—A
> FIELD OF FORCE

that is, that, as agent of this collective (which ORIGIN is going to be) the question is larger than, yr taste, alone: it is the same sort of confrontation as—in any given poem—a man faces: how much energy has he got in, to make the thing stand on its own feet as, a force, in, the fields of force which surround everyone of us, of which we, too, are forces: to stand FORTH

This is getting to sound altogether too much like the PV thing! And altogether too theoretical, goddamn it, a demonstrandum, ahead of time! But do not be put off, cid.
> What I am getting at, is, that, you've got one hell of a headache on yr head, and i am trying to give you the best of my perception for, whatever use it may be, ahead. That is, two things struck me about ORIGIN 1:

that, because the space of a magazine is so (finally) small—*close*—a run of many men & women's pieces (no matter how good they are, if they are professional alone) tend to cancel each other out, that is, that you get something you never get when you are inside one person's work (a book, say), you get subjects, and even images, neutralizing each other! It's crazy, but, in fact, you get what is the force of taste knocking itself out against the expression, next page, of another force of taste!

Now, I don't in any sense, think this is fault—either theirs, or, yrs.
It merely raises up the whole question, how, can one make a mag WORK?

And, I get back to the notion that—as any live thing—it is a question of
how the units are juxtaposed so that they declare (stand in the place of)
the man who puts them together

In other words, that, yr problem as editor, is, to find out how to (omit,
even!), *what* to put together so that, each unit keeps its force and, at
the same time, the whole mag lives

it is this *what,* that puts the whole thing, hard: questions—
(1) in
the small space of an issue of a mag frankly "for the creative", how much
variation of materials can one get in (does one have to keep in) to save all
units from mutual cancellation?

You already know my guesses as to roads toward, the answer: that is, the
most obvious, is, to *broaden the base*
and i don't mean simply to, say,
all the arts.   On the contrary.

I'd guess, that the answer here, is, has to be, YOU: that is, for you to
get in, to any given issue, as close to all the possible angles to a given
issue that you can conceivably think of—which means that you yrself
are *the packed one,* eh?

Nor do I think it is as complicated as I make it sound, if one could get
to a series of principles for the governance of, any of us going in that
common direction, today

And here again you know my own biases: that is, (1), keep clear of the
insides of, any assumptions which are a part of, or colored by "Western",
or "Christian", history
(2) which means most of our assumptions abt
taste and "the aesthetics of" any art (as proceeding fr, the Greeks, &
first formulated significantly by Aristotle, and Longinus, etc.

(3) offset to 1 & 2, kinetics of
contemporary physics, say, as more healthful than, either of above, and
of the *graphic* as a better runner for the sleigh or cart than, humanism

Well, this is beginning to run down.   All I felt was, that, I owed you
all my first thoughts abt, the problems that, ORIGIN now presents—now

that she is out there, to be seen, done, bless you, and damned wonder-
fully *ahead*.   And I owed it to you, simply because you have already gone
so far: in fact I rather think the job is to push what you have already
started (as to the devices of presentation) even further—that is, the one
man, the book, the juxtaposition of varying materials, or varying devices,
thicken, thicken, PACK, in order to set aside any lingering results of
"literary" or "aesthetics" or "professional" orderings (what i have here
dubbed "Taste" dangers, and, in so doing, seen as inherited culture
patterns which, a magazine devoted, as yrs is, to fresh energies, has
to cut away. . . .

52

lerma, campeche, mexico   [8 May 51]

cid:

  . . . Well, lad, am in a turmoil, these days, with, the necessity to:
move on!   (Black Mt has offered me the summer post, again—and it is
tempting, with friend Ben Shahn to be there in July, and Katy Litz, to
be the dance lady the whole time: than whom, fr what she has done to my
lads & girls there, last summer, must be just about the only dancer
there is, these days, who is moving, forward:
                                          which is another idea,
for *origin*, ahead: an investigation into, the whole question of, where
is dance, as an *art*, now: it could be very exciting, and i cld get you
stuff fr katy, & merce cunningham, and my boy nick cernovich (there)
whose work is the very best i know fr a man under 20 (verse, music,
dance; he did a dance (quite without my knowledge) to a poem of mine
on the death of a guy in a sub, which was beautiful (this winter).   And
has picked up fr me on drama as dance to do a (what they call a noh)
dance, now.   i don't

as well as (another tie, which, these glyphs ---) jesus: you shld see
what movements, gestures, investivations of nature these glyphs, contain!

                      well, for you, and delight still under
                the light of Origin ♯1!

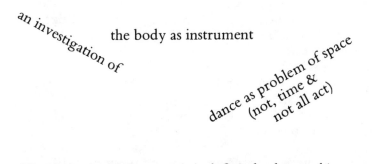

      That is (written) dance as it is definitely the *graphic*
        of drama (mime, as only the broader aspect of
          gesture &, motion
    (voice (verse) as working against, & out
        of, such, under motion ---- dance as
        motion *around* language

dictum: any player is (has to be) 1st dancer

cid:
          two letters fr you just in, which, added to one last week un-
answered, make it imperative I at least tell you—
                                        for you must excuse
me: i was asked now 12 days ago to do a statement of what i have been
up to here, and what i would propose to do if i was given money—and god
help me there is nothing harder in this life for me to do than to make such
statements—and now, the problem is even greater than it ever was,
simply because my own prose ways (say, G & C) have to be broken back
to the universe of discourse, and that, is unbearable
                                        —so night & day
i try and try to state the thing, and it boggles, is not
what i want

          (you see, it has not been sufficiently observed, particu-
larly in our own time, that reason & the art of comparison are a stage
which a man must master, but, are not what our world takes them to
be, final discipline: they wear the false face.   For beyond them is direct
perception and contraries, which dispose of argument.   But such a movement forward is very difficult for a rational society to comprehend,
implying, as it does, a circular concept of life.   That is, the harmony
of the universe is not logical, or, better, is post- or supra-logical.
As is the order of any created things.
                              I am most impatient with
argument & logic, not because i do not believe in same—in fact I
trained myself from the age of 14 on, in just such, until, by 20, i
was starting to walk down (as a letter carrier, thus, with much chance
to walk down!) the *appetites* which argument & reason create.   But to
this very day I have not broken beyond to anything like a sustained
life in the universe beyond the universe of discourse (and I don't
mean at all any asiatic passivism).   I mean that there is a temptation
of the mind which also has to be thrown back, thrown, in.
                                        In fact,
Lawrence, here, is the one to the point—that, he saw the temptation,
and put the mind back in to the pot.
                              I have fed as much on a remark of
Blake's as on any single remark of any man: Oppositions are not true
contraries.

Well, lad, just to let you know, to thank you for all yr news, to tell
you I gave you, in my list, the best store of possible moneys i could,
and to urge you not to be discouraged: I think you are way out ahead
of what is the usual invasion of the American lethargy in such matters....
And please keep the letters coming at me, even if it means only, that
you wish to groan aloud!

Cid—
          yr fine letter has just come in, and because today *only*, now for
three weeks, have I not been at this report (it is now something for the
gods only to sit to, as Board, of Trustees!   —or I should send it to you
for Origin!
               truth is, though it has been straight suffering, because it is
both too early & too late to do it, yet, in the doing, I have straightened out
several problems of glyph procedure, & of application of my own aesthetic
generally

the art of the language of glyphs
IS
motion in time on stone

picked up sore throat, had bad night, & today am dosed with 666 "seis
seis seis" says the ball games, broadcast, here instead of sharp sharp
sharp

so I take this moment (not knowing, the way I stubbornly refuse to discharge
this petition until i have managed to poise it exactly between me, & them,
like you say, directly
                              Oregon, I *think*, was, if you know oregon like
                              I know oregon, you'd, I think, think that it is
                              still (the coast!) strangely frontier, where, a
                              streetcar is as it was when it was NEW, a lovely
                              Toy, open car, seats crosswise all the width,
                              "Today,"
                                        with a radio in every
                              car, & all white
                                   satin like the finest
                              shit, for
                              burying the

the point is
          delighted to hear you will be setting me in there, 2, with
lad Bob—
               & *yes*, do put A Po-sy . . .
                                        for one thing I think the poem will
teach these fools, this which the others should teach them (especially
the guy who thot I thot I was pulling off some ree-volt(ing) to tell a
tone from a pose, eh?
               a POZ-
Y!
          love that little one for,
its gayety, tho Con (mia esposa from the first sd, she
liked it cause,
personally bitter!

Please write.   And it will reach me.   Carlos, the carrier here, is muy amable.   Siempre....

Cid: Thank you.   Glad you wrote me here.   For I stay on.   My reason now
is, work of my own.   Verse.   Or the hope for same: a feeling that, if I
idle, something is making.   One never knows, but, when I have this sort
of feeling—anticipation—I obey.
                        It probably means I shall not get over
to Mexicó, that, instead, I shall go directly from here to Black Mt (where
I am tentative due July 8th: they have asked me to do the summer writing
job, and for some crazy reason I want to—perhaps it is the fact that Ben
Shahn and Katy Litz will be there, too.   As well that several of the men
and women whom I took fresh now three years ago will be winding up next
year—and there are a couple of them whom I think you yŕself will be
interested in soon.   It is now a money question: fare.

Let me hold off on answering you on the glyphs for just a bit, until I set
it all formally down for you, as a go, for Origin, eh?   I am anxious to
do it, but I shall need the second drive here (in the fall, I hope—and
that time, in Guatemala and at Copan).
                        But there is one shot broke on
me this week.   I had picked up, the day before, from a dealer, a carved
animal snout with the original red paint on it.   I think it was that piece
which made my leap come.   For you may recall that the worship of
Priapus in the Mediterranean civilization included the painting of the
huge phalluses which were centered in gardens, & by the roads, *red*.
At the same time you may also remember that Greek sculpture in the
round appears to have emerged from the *herms,* the single heads of
Hermes which were at crossroads & such in earliest Greece.   Now these
herms, the assumption is, were originally phalluses, which, as sophist-
ication came on, were rounded, at the glans penis, into heads, Hermes
head predominantly.

It is difficult to reify this, now, because none of us, now, find it easy to
take a phallus as an image (i have a hunch we reverse the ancients, and
make metaphors out of bananas and such rather than, as they, make the
phallus, in a sense, a metaphor.   For my assumption is that they took
the phallus—& sex—as simply man's most immediate way of knowing
nature's powers—and the handiest image of that power.   For example,
to make this point one needs also to keep in mind the tremendous image
that a snake was (someday, have a look at Jane Harrison's plates of
the snake, & Zeus, in her PROLOGOMENA TO GREEK RELIGION.   She
shies away from the full import, but, enough is there to recognize that the
snake, and the phallus were, together, of immense resonance for early
Mediterranean man (which, as you know, I take to be evidence that, through
Sumeria, the same was true for all man's earliest civilization.)

Now.   What turns out to be—again—the hidden thing here ((why do these
historians *hide* such matters?   Ezra can cry that history leaves out the

manipulations of credit, and I will agree, but what seems to me an even
more overwhelming erasure is, the hiding of sex as force through some
phoney Christian concept of pudor)), is the multiple evidence of the
importance of the phallus in the *city* life of

the MAYA

((it is but another mark of the extraordinary intellectual
clarity of the New Englanders of 1835-1855 that it is in John Stephens'
description of Uxmal (in his "Travels in Yucatan", 1843—which I
would suggest you read for the direct pleasure of same—) that I found
the most important clue of all
rather, I had found it myself at Uxmal,
and, in trying to find anyone who reported same, the only man whom I
did find was Stephens—and since he "found" the place more examples
of these huge phalluses centered to the front of the most important
buildings—the Governor's Palace, and the so-called Nun House—were
then standing than I could now find

What makes this important is, that Uxmal is *later*, rather, that these
buildings are late (for at both Uxmal, and Chichen Itza, in what is now
called the "old" parts, there are literally phallic temples—at Uxmal,
for example, the funniest thing of all—they used phalluses for rain
spouts! gargoyles!!

But the phalluses I refer to, and Stephens does, are late, are not direct
phallic repros, but are huge monoliths, obviously central to the public
life as late as 1200 AD

Which gets me home.   For what I am now beginning to think is, that
the *stelae* (you called them totem poles, which they also are): and
what are totem poles?)   are *herms*!
That, sometime about 300—maybe
earlier if, as I also surmise, all this use of erected monoliths for record
in stone was preceded by same monuments in *wood* ((again, the relation
to earliest Greece—the wood E, at Delphi))
(((this whole wood question
is tremendously important, and also, like sex, ducked by the investigators:
for it explains the *complicated* & ornate carving of stone at the very
beginning of the glyph art, and it also explains why the Maya *painted*
their *stones* throughout their history)))

anyway, that, very early, the Maya *transposed* the phallus to the stela:
it accounts for one thing no one has sd much about, that the stela were
worshipped—one of the earliest of all, at Uaxactun, is all burned from the
copal offerings laid at its base!
as well as it accounts for two other things:

(1) that the stelae are given a principal place in the architectural plan—
are placed where the huge phalluses are at Uxmal; and (2) that they are
usually related to "altars" of their own, where, apparently, some sort
of rites were done

This is almost all new stuff, so far as I have been able to check.   Of course it
may be that I am only the first one to put it in writing—historians usually knowing more than they say, thereby invalidating their responsibility to others, &
making them creatures to be damned.   And you must allow me to say these things
to you tentatively, until I have been to more sites, & seen with my own eyes
what they don't tell me are there.   But the harmony of these observations to
experience elsewhere makes sense of them.   ((I meant, above, to make the
point that, the suppression of all such information is one of the reasons why
poor Lawrence, who was actually only another accurate man, was heaped with
so much infamy by the hiders and the prurient.))

   The other thing which interested me in yr letter, was yr observation that
good prose was not coming in.   It made its point the more on me that I had,
this week, read all of New Directions XII.   Now I do not mean to make too
much of ND.   But as a sampling of present prose it reinforces an impression
I have had bearing also on what you yrself say abt the younger men.   Did Bob
ever happen to show you the introductory notes i did on narrative in re his
stories called OUTSIDE, INSIDE?   Not that it matters, only, there, I had sd,
that I took it that now, prose narrative had to go only either of two ways.   And
what impresses me is, that *every* piece in Laughlin's is either standing still
(the realism, of Lowery, of an able young guy named John Lawson, of an equally
able Italian named Monicelli—all of which is that "psychological realism" which
Melville should have called a halt on, that Stendhal and the others after him
had done up enough) or it is downright reactionary.   And it is this latter class of
stuff which deeply discloses the conditions which, I'd bet, are leaving you
without any prose to print.   For most of ND XII is made up of narrative which
is nothing more than de Maupassant (Elliot Stein's Confessions of a Young
Insomniac), necrophilism (bad Poe: Paul Bowles' Dona Faustina—and, a
curious combination of same & realism, John Hawkes' Death of an Airman),
and WW Jacobs' The Monkey's Claw!   (perhaps the most skillful of all, Jack
Dunphy's Under the African Trees).
                              I mean, literally, that the *forms* of
narrative have reacted back from the advances of Joyce, say, to these earlier
& poorer men, and at the same time, the substance is without any of the
rationale which made de Maupassant, Poe, and Jacobs excusable.   For these
men—all, more or less, creatures of Tennessee Williams' invocation—are
ducking their own times, and choosing to make public their own psychic de-
rangements as though they were thus proving the time!   Which, of course, is
not so much their fault as that other men are not showing them up for what they

are—as you know, I think Bob is the *only* narrative writer I know now at work who is doing just that, who is a responsible writer.

The worst group of reaction therein is the derivative of Kafka—and when anything is not by Kafka it comes out most like Thomas Mann! The classic of this, in ND XII, is a Philip Siekevitz's The Fish—good jesus god, you should read that! all about the river Bios! ow. And, of course, there is existenz: Maurice Toesca's Indirect Suicide.

Well, no use saying more. Just nothing in the whole collection: nothing. And what a comment that is.
                    But don't give up yr own resistance. For I should reinforce you: you should, rather, be surprised if you get *any* prose narrative except from Bob! Not that you won't get it. But you will have to be patient. Narrative writing is, at the moment, wholly waiting for the advance of verse. Only the poets now can pull the narrative writers ahead. The situation of 1910 (post-Flaubert) is reversed, as well as the plane has shifted. Then it was quite true what Ford first said, and Ezra gave circulation to: that verse should be at least as well written as prose. The revolution has done its work. The proposition now is, that prose must handle narrative by juxtaposition as accurate as verse. For *all* narrative now is hung up on the question of *content*: how to manage reality by other means than (1) the psychological, (2) the psychic as the night-of-the-soul (which comes out shit & necrophilism, due to psychoanalysis inadequately transposed by inaccurate writers), (3) external, or social reality, which comes out either Hemingwayism (Lowery & his school—the phoney American cinematic realism, document in the false sense, but which is, even at that, the most powerful thing we are getting: an example, here, is William Inge, who, in ND XII, has a job of bobby-sox autograph hunters called "For Bobolink, for her Spirit" the twin to which I read in a February Sat Eve Post!
                    or, some social realism, the Kafka Mann Rosenfeld stuff—the flight from communism into a Graustark never never land.

No, don't be discouraged. Allow a few poets to get their work done in yr pages, and then prose will begin to come in. In fact Origin 2, by way of Creeley, ought to begin the push. Give that issue a while to get around, and some characters somewhere will see what he's up to with his conjecture. For Creeley is the push beyond Lawrence. And Lawrence is the *only* predecessor who can carry narrative ahead.
                    ((i would be interested, for example, to hear from you if *any* mss you have received shows any learning fr Lawrence.))

Well, for today. And thanks.

                    You can't imagine how much joy I have that

you are planning to put Po-Sy in there (and not the least of the reasons is, that, there, there are relations to the above problems—how you give man motion in terms of his story

((((one quick note: motion is *not* time.   That is, at each of its extremes, time takes on more the nature of space.   You forget they are one: space-time.   And that, depending on the position and the mass of either, we read them more one or the other.   For example, past time, at its outer limits—or present time, e.g., stretched at night by stars—does not, to our senses, move.   The extension is so great that, given the law of our senses, the *effect* is—like a design— instantaneous, and thus, because we take it in at once, is, static— though this is a false word, and if I replace it by plastic, I think you will see more clearly what I intend.   For example, circular motion (or cyclical) is plastic, as against time as a progression

((how frightfully important the absence of this comprehension is, is the case of Eberhart, who can say to you I am repetitious. I recently read many pages of him, and found not one phrase or line which was his own—in the sense that, it was this man, & no other, disclosing his experience.   On the contrary, his "variety" is mere eclecticism, a running over of things by a series of cliches which—like any cliche—come from other men.   E.g., no rhythmic perception whatsoever.   He has never learned lesson ♯1:   that he who has rhythm has the universe.))

And when I sd motion in time on stone I meant that at this extreme—the instant—time is inseparable from space, and so an individual glyph is seized by the eye in such a small interval of time that one can speak of it as motion inside of time
                it is the glyph-block, and whole stone that, like a relief, or a mural, or a Chinese scroll, has to be measured in time—the eye has to move narratively

I press in with this because the whole reason why you are not getting prose narrative is involved with this problem: writers are terribly behindhand, in not discovering, as Cavalcanti discovered the physics of light in his time, the important bearing on their own work of the relativism of space-time concept. . . .

Lerma,   Sunday,   June 17 (?)

My dear Cid:

    Well.   I'm shooting along to you—as promised—what looks like
the first result of work, eh?
                            A curious one, but it was damned fun
to write (and a damn good feeling it was to have Origin there to be
writing it toward, I can tell you).
                            If you like it, and it sits there a
while, I dare say I will want to put my hand on to it again (as I did
with G & C).   But I want you to have it now, to have a look—in any
case, to be yours back, for the part you played in it, telling me that
prose was what you were missing!   and that you were going to study
philosophy this summer!

    Do write.   Miss hearing from you.   And I think now I can be
pretty definite: we will hang on here, the money is so gone, until just
about July 2nd or 3rd, when our expectation is that we can get a free
ride by lumber boat over to Pensacola.   From there we will drag
ourselves by bus direct to Black Mt.   They have asked me to return,
as I guess I told you, to do their summer writing job.   And as I have
no other way to support myself, I will.   On top of that, it turned out
I had to be affiliated with some institution in order to get a crack at the
stake I hope to have to return here September 1st, or thereabouts, to
continue the glyph book—and to get you all the Sanchez stuff, both
for O and for the exhibition.

    So you can reach me here up to almost the 1st, and, thereafter,
Black Mt College, Black Mt., North Carolina.

    Funniest damn thing, the way it has all worked out.   Will hate
to leave here: we are now getting the increment.   All the people know
us, some are our friends.   Spanish is now usable, and if I could stay
right on, the Maya would come roaring home.   And all the pleasures
of being a part of one's ambience is flooding in.   It is very good.

    Well, here, Olson, and his

                                        affections

        the question of act
     1st determinant of
            value
     acts are value

                            [mss of "Human Universe" enclosed]

62

cid.   Next to last day.   And I have two fullsome letters of yrs in front
of me—including a quote fr Santayana (the 2nd) which i have taken
something from, don't know what.   But it swirls in those places i enjoy,
eh?   and you were acute, to shoot it to me.   my thanks, for it and all.

What you repeat, is this biz, of moneys for ♯4, and it stays on my mind,
tho what help i can be in such matters, beyond what I did in giving you
my own friends, for levy, i don't know.   look: i have been thinking about
it, and tho i haven't come up with anything very bright, let me talk abt it:

above all, don't get discouraged, by subscriptions or by such silence as
the heaviest of all, the pound's.   for maybe you yrself don't remember
what a push ORIGIN is, how far it does go away from what has been.
And that it's force, shall have to gather its own way behind it.   They won't
come running, any of them.   But my own impression—and it's not merely
from the ride you are giving me—my own serious impression is, that you
are literally the mag which was called for, and which does show already
the push beyond what has been.   (Ex: set yrself against NINE, and see
how, instead of, as they, and the tendency of all the new American
magazines, is *reactionary*, is back toward tradition, and a whole series
of cliche positions—and at such a time.   Typically, political, in their sources!

that is, don't be fearful of 4 before november, no matter how much you
are right to push now, for 4—for example, ♯2 should ride you further,
what with Bob (who is certainly the most important narrative writer to
come on in one hell of a time, and is, to my taking, the push beyond
Lawrence—which is something, for certainly Pound and Lawrence more
and more stand up as the huge two of the 1st half of the 20th century...

you see, with 2 or 3 issues out, you will be seen to be a serious character
(i am speaking from all buyers' hesitancies, not from myself—i know you
are, but they—they have seen too many little mags pop up, suddenly
start coming at long intervals, and die: by getting ♯2 out July 15, on
schedule, and ♯3 October 15, you will have already shown them you mean
business, and it is just about then that they will have to take you seriously,
and that subs should rise (the fall, too, and all that)...

Have written Nancy Leonard, saying, fer chrissake, see Cid gets MR1.
For if you don't know Kingfishers you don't have a starter!   And In cold
Hell—know that?   it's the big brother of For Sappho- and I am so damned
mad it has stayed dead in Emerson's hand for a year, it is enough to lead
me to the courts!   For I can't think of anything outside your purvieu I
should rather have you have!

And you shall have THE CAUSE (the one I sd I was holding for you: just
let me keep it a little longer—it's a sort of fetish.   And the two long ones

I have already sent you, in the past couple of weeks, plus HU, let
you know I am alive, eh?..

Even paper done in!   we have figured things so close!   What a time it
has been—holding, waiting for words, letters, even for checks—and
going along down to the very edge of this low-lying boat now sitting
there (we can see it, from our patio!   what a way to travel—from yr
own front door, direct!) waiting to take us on with the rest of the
lumber.

And keep coming at me, there, BMC:

64

cid:

     please bear with me a short time more—all yr good mail is
in hand (Lerma, and here)—and i am only prevented by two
things
         (1) that, working into the loss of time working for our
             board and room takes, is cutting me down on the
             chances to write you

     & (2) that the above is true only because the pace of my own
             writing of June continues: so i have to rob you as Cid
             in order to pay you as Ed!

                    I AM REWRITING HU FOR *YOU*

been at it since arrival—since last thursday—in & out—and just
because if, find it more and more my base, my bedrock, it is the
harder and the more interesting!

     so, take this, as sign, and please keep it coming at me:
as well as origin 2—as well, if you could spare it, *fragmente*
(which i would return: no sign or word of my own copy anywhere!)

        will be back on, directly

65

CID CORMAN,   *EDITOR*,   ORIGIN

I have just two minutes ago finished reading Miss Hoskins' lovely
sad (and as sad, wrong) but lovely poem.   Since then I have thumbtacked
your dollar bill (now my dollar bill) on my wall at my back alongside
the chart of the Gulf of Mexico and adjoining lands the skipper of the
Bennestvet Brovig sent me for a present.   And I am about to say this:
that if you ain't *the god damn best editor* since when

                                        (since ever such

leading on a dance of mss, such a man
to compose a collective?   where, has there been, such
a man as Cid
corman—core-
man (chore-
agos)?

          God, it moves me, this issue (more, surely, more, it is, more
than ♯1, in just this, plus, that, here, this Creeley, this wonder lad, is
the whole show—god, how, so far (not all yet read) how, his SUMMER
and his NOTES

          you see, Cid, I would send you back the dollar . . I would send
you millions. . . . I do not know why the world does not see that here,
this ORIGIN, by the hand of (the taste of . . the will of   this corman
    IS   what is it to be compared to?
                              I grant, that, because it is (you
must permit us to say this pride, too) *ours,* i am somewhat blind.   Sure.
BUT, I have also—do not lose—my judgment (cannot, it has taken too
many years to be even floated off in this joy you have now twice given me
—and this ♯2 is even a greater joy for me: why, I honestly think,
because you have here cleaned down to, such clean mss, and, my lad,
how, he shines, eh?

for example, this miss hoskins mss is the finest of hers (you are right
to think so), so delicate, so sad, so, wrong

. . . and were one creeley and one olson ever joined *before*—or shall
they *ever* be so joined again, the fall
of the COCK, just, where you have laid it in, between others, thus
poised, rightly, off Creeley, and yet, between him more than between
these others?   (I cannot see how, that piece, of mine, could, placed
as you have placed it, carry, any more power, going, as it goes straight
from where our lad, in SUMMER, goes fr Lawrence—does not there yet
know what Lawrence does, in what I have sd reads to me more true now
than when I sd it—but is going, when, after his NOTES (which comes

handily, fr SUMMER and my COCK, following after them) he will, he
does, he can, he will and how he will move on even from Lawrence, in
MR BLUE, the beginning of, his full seizure of, ACTION (his door, he
is through it, the door of SUMMER, the door of the quadrangle two sides
of which, the two sides which had to be measured by him first, and are
now here measured: time, & memory—how, he has mastered this
opening of, such a man as he, his house

(I must make tale & point here, of a remarkable accident of type which I
 also insist you took account of, your composing, is of such an order:

     pages 74 and 75 lie together as though a god walked across them

And though Cantar de Noit, and the Bereaved, are of an order too poetic
for my taste
         (who sd, paint that smells of paint?)
                      ((I say, you save all
by having the sense, the common fruitful sense, god love you, to put
the GOAT LETTER—my god, doesn't he say it to you, as, surely, he
didn't say it to me, or anybody, how, exactly, it drops!))

((I have left fr p 110 to later, just, because, two times now, it has
  been an ultimate pleasure to lie down on that bed and read this
magazine of your own making . . . yesterday, and now again today, in
the midst of work (some of it continuing to go on with HU, for you,
the next), to knock off, and take up this pretty thing
                      (((the colors
         of the cover are, so much more attractive, this
         time—and again, i like your personal note, &
         find also your characterizations or, locations,
         of yr people much improved

my GOD, CID, has any one told you, what a hell of a wonderful leading
on of his own work it is to have it looking like this?   I will, then, for
one tell you, that the company you cause me to keep—the way you put
all of us down together—the quality of what you put down beside me makes
me drive on HU with a different drive, with more, even, than I, alone, . . .
with this publication ahead, you cause me to tone up even my own toned
up will!

so why shldn't I ask, where, was there ever such, an editor, where?

(as Ford, for DHL, & Ez, and Hardy, those first days, the English Review?

     which seems to me to spot you, if there is a spot (and you'd well
     guess, I don't even think—those days—were days as crucial as
     our own!)

if there is any gauge of what you are here doing, i doubt there is, for
to put a PERKOFF beside c and me, by god, who, has had that width except

well, only poets, the finest, have, such a sense for, the proper
juxtaposition, the world taste to, keep it this lean and make it fat!

to make a hell of the proper parts is dante business—and to give a
magazine some of such?

And don't be scared of this enthusiasm, think it is such, and tomorrow...
no: it is already tomorrow, and I sit square, and hard to this: all that
I've said.   And I take it no fault of yrs that, ISSUE MOOD, does, seem,
losing some margin the mss had, not quite as clear a bit of music as
the mss was—some vertical hunching it should not have, printed, another
time.   But this is learning, and I do not make it fault: it is only, that
it took me myself two readings to understand it!

No, cid, all all here, is done with nicest (nice, in its fine sense)
discrimination:
                        yr ability to move fr a base of feeling to include a
Perkoff all the way to the will to bring about such a magazine and move
it money-wise and all wise,
                        by such composition make it *STAND*

                                it is wonderful, no less than
                                a damned MIRACLE
        & thanks for yr letter, just in?

            jump, you
            bitch, pimp
            the world is yr
            mother—but
            hasn't tamed you yet
    my father was a Job
    but not such a Job
    as that.   He kept
            the dog-
            eared animal
            that guards
            the gates such
            well-ordered gates are
            meant to be entered
            and reentered,
                    are)

68

cid:

    ...the rewrite of HU is giving me major excitement, & is fine,
just because the pull of it (as of June 1) is still on me—so, what
you shall have, may, or may not, differ decidedly from what you
have.   Of course you were quite right about the context of ND—that
went out of it, the 1st day.   And yr words on laws, has caused me
to sharpen what i mean by same—tho, I could not remove this concept
without deeply erasing my own base ((if you will have noted how, at the
end of G & C, it is laws I quote, as pre-Hammurabi)).   On this, I
think I shall content you—in fact, this new stuff is much more exciting

the point is, what was there, is, finally, my base—i have, here,
set my cultural position.   And so, it is a rasslin, this rewrite.
There is, here, the body, the substance, of my faith.   And so, it
is very exciting to me, and I shall want to make it good for you,
for 3

    A hell of a lot of verse keeps coming.   But you have some
big ones there, and I shall hold what is in hand for yr future?—well,
perhaps i'll make you a copy of one, for it just might seem such an
offset to what you have published of mine that it will teach Bronk and
Morse and whoever (including Miss Hoskins) or all neo-classicists,
who it is who can practice what they so jingoistically preach

                    it is called A ROUND   (for Katy Litz
                                              &
                    A CANON   (for Lou Harrison

    I am so sick of this sort of thing you show me from Bronk-
the green of it, the green-sick, too—the bad-headedness, as well
as the manners...

    i am particularly incensed—not as of his remarks on me, which,
who but, just the few of us, isn't making, and isn't likely to continue
to make?   who, actually, reads me—that is, repeats the reading—it
is again, as I sd abt the German critic you quoted me: the confusion of
the tone for the mode
                    i am more aware than either such, or Bronk,
what, the appearance is—the idiots, to be so easy about it, eh?
((for me, the test of any of em, is, The Story of O!   that's what they
  ought to look twice at, eh?   And I can tell you, I am mighty proud
  of you that, you, without saying a word, put that one, into print!
  For, for my money, there, all their cracks melt—cute, eh....

HOW MANY PEOPLE EVEN HAVE THE INTELLIGENCE TO READ
    THE (for MAGAZINE also read) THE POEM AS IT IS PUT TOGETHER?

returns in falsehood
heart's hoighted bright
    in chill,
    in pain
numb-songed & wisdomless

my dear cid:
     i'll start this letter
on this start of a poem
just to prove to you how very
squeezed time is for me here,
so that you will forgive me
my delay in not answering
three fullsome letters from
you.   For these lines were set down the evening I went to tell Harrison
& Litz the very satisfying news, that you welcomed their poem and
will fire it straight between the eyes of the other two in ♯3

                for that surely is the finest
news, the most delightful news has come my way this last week: i am
overwhelmingly gratified

the truth is, tho i do lose just that time one has when one does not
have to spend a few hrs each day making the wife 's & yr own board
& room, (tho i can't write the letters i want to), to you, because i
have to spend those hrs on these students, YET
                        there are several
good things come, and yesterday, was one such culmination:

(1)   a guy named Larry Hat (who came here two weeks ago) (((i have
       told him all about you, showed him the 2 ORIGINS, and he has
       been very interested, because he is a trained lithographer from
       San Francisco by way of the Chicago Inst of Design))) walked
       in 6:00 with the finished dummy of a new Olson work!   a new work
       yet undone, but you should see the handsome thing he has put out
       —and now i have to write it!   a few days verse, to finish it,
       and i won't say any more, but have one of the special 25 copy
       edition for you

(2)   but to keep him busy designing the next few days, i toyed with
       a little book of poems, to be called, BLACK MT POEMS, and to
       be a handful done here the past month—but i gave that idea up,
       because i felt that you should have all things, and clear, for
       first printing, even tho anything printed here is "local" and "limited"

(3)   instead, i had the wild idea, to take the LETTER TO BE READ *AWAY*
       FROM the Centenary Celebration of Melville's Moby-Dick at Williams
       College Labor Day Weekend (it was written, in a moment of flame,
       two weeks ago), and fire it as a bit of verse pamphleteering
       (something I don't know has been much done since the Elizabethans)
       and by god if the kids last night didn't raise the 20 bucks to
       have it set by electrotype in Caslon, so that we can sell it at
       that damned stupid celebration, and also sell it as an olson poem!

So, today, I imagine Hat, and Vanderbeek, and others are over
in Asheville arranging the biz, and here am I confronted with
the necessity to rewrite it!

BUT now, telling you all this, must seem to you to be keeping me from
my proper last, of preparing anything and all things for you!   for
ORIGIN 3!   Which is not quite true, for, each day now, for all these
weeks, I have added, and added, to the simplicity of the LAWS of the
HU.   And why I write you the above, is only to see if—what you yrself
propose in yr last letter—can be worked out.

Let me put it this way:

I am quite anxious   (1)   to finish HU
                (2)   to lay it home, there, in ♯3
                (3)   to make it a sort of huge & simple piece of
                      Mosaic stone

And my impression is, that, it is the frame of these 8 weeks, and
should be so done—as an organic act.   For I think I told you that I
read it as my first act here, and propose to read it, rewritten, as
my last.

      . . . I still have to rewrite the Melville (it's only value is
this immediate time proposition—like all polemic—that it be published *before* these idiots meet) and have to write originally the *A of T*

AND THAT BOTH HAVE TO BE DONE (so far as my part goes) BY
THE END OF THIS WEEK!

                      So, we are in the clear, perhaps, on
HU—that is, I will have two full weeks before yr deadline.
                              Just, if
you think you could let me have that other two weeks as well if I shld
need them, let me know
                well, thank you for everything, and *please*
keep writing to me: i miss hearing more often all news, and doings

                    (by the way,
i have found out, from Larry Hat, Rob't Duncan's friend's address,
and have written Duncan to send you something

Monday   Sept 3   [BMC]

CID: if you will now know that i have, *in the past week*, overseen the
        design and printing (and actually wrote one) of two projects (one
        enclosed as present for you)
                            at the same time I was ill with a
        cracked rib (baseball!)
                            that Con's mother died at 53 in Boston
        a week ago last night
                            that during that week I was finishing the 8
        week stretch here that also i was asked to stay here this year,
        and had to make up my mind (still damn well NOT made up)

        that i have had people and people and people at me, night & day,
        and no chance

                    well, as Miss Shoolman must have told you, I
        was so upset at not managing to get to this machine to tell you
        how very tremendously that invitation you sent us for her rode
        us—and at such a time that we needed just such a ride!

                    that I was in the booth once, to call you (the night *before* I
        had her wire
                    and had to give it up because—goddamn it—i just
        couldn't afford the 1. 75 for same!)

SO PLEASE, Cid, just allow me that crush, and figure, that, your very
deep act was something so wonderful that, I am still sort of alive with it,
wanting it . . .

        But here's the hitch, or the two hitches:

1) We do not have the means to travel (nor, in Con's case, perhaps, the
doctor's okay—she is expecting, as of October 19) ((At the same time she
is urging me to take a vacation.   But I will not, at least until I have THE
HU   rewrite done for you!))

&2) that, actually, such a move to New England ought—would almost
have to—be the alternative to staying here for four-five months (last
week, they offered me an appointment, for this year, which I have not
accepted yet—as you know, I believe in the Chinese system, of an
active man living where life is, & coming to youth once a month   NOT,
living in the midst of them, as, here—*dread it, dread—fear it!*
The damnable thing is

1) I won't know, until after Sept 15, whether the NY people are going to
   give me the grant to continue the Maya work on the ground

&2) that, until that decision is made, I have (according to the conditions of their board) to be "affiliated with an institution"...

It boils down to this:
                    that only here am I
one (1) somewhat self-supporting
& (2) (for two weeks to a month) satisfying the conditions to get this
            grant which will enable me to finance life for a couple of years
            (the exchange value in Mexico is such)

BUT   I don't relish staying here the full fall term.   I shall have to
    (ethically), would so much like rather to be there, my home
    coming, N. E.

Well Cid, this is the best answer I am capable of at this moment, to
yr generous offer.   Don't honestly know what to do

                One thing, anyway.   I'm falling in,
    tomorrow, on HU, for you!

                Please write--& I shall

73

CID

       yr fine letter just in, and, because i am trying to get on
top of everything (now that the bizness of this place is a little off
my back: :: :

                 they did the whole thing, and sd, as of my
                 staying, stay as long or as little as you
                 want, and then, when you wish to do other-
                 wise, well we'll figure it out
                                   can't
                 ask for more, eh?

as a matter of fact, have taken this week, to breathe, clean up
papers, square away for the go on HU—
          am taking it, you can give me until the 15th
          God be wi me, that, in the next week, I can set it
          cool

Have not seen C's GRACE, but sent you yesterday, as he asked, his
new PARTY, and, for me, it is again ON—the attack, and the form,
are beautiful, a subtle, lovely, light running thing, and full of fate
& power (he is such a beautiful thing, that lad, what he bears in on—
and with)
          and i am not surprised his issue bombed them—the only
thing i can't figure out is, why there shld be any controversy!
Can't they see?

And I am very grateful for yr moving around ES.   It is damned nice
to be reinforced so, just now, when, things (economic things) are so
multiplied—not that it's the having of, a baby: such a thing seems
so much non-economic to a character like myself, so much just
what it is, that thing, the act of, and my lady so cool and solid (and
beautiful in it, with it), that I (and of course I never had much real-
istic—I think they call it—sense of future::::always go along with
life, not, throw ahead, like some highway, knowing where it goes
(where does it, go?)

So, it's openeyed, sort of stuff. No. The thing is, because *Origin*
exists, I write better, I write more,—and any economic consequence
(even to the buck you sent which is pinned to the wall, as well as any
such action that ES may choose to take) just makes the whole thing
have the sort of sense that, say, Con having a baby makes
                                      makes solids
(and the lord knows any of us who, take ourselves and throw ourselves
in the air like leaves—or stones—like, to have something, come down,
fall, solid, back
               instead of staying luftsmensch (as they are, in, say

Warsaw, or, Naples, or Montmartre: un grec)

what you have
given me is, such solid.   And that ES is aware, is like, in a
different way, eh?
((These two things: print, and money for, work
they are, the dream, what?))

. . . well, just quick

My dear Cid:

breaking off, from the mss of HU, to get you a note, figuring, if you are holding for me—for it—you shld know the present state—length—and when you can look for it

i cracked the worst of it (the opening pages) today, after several days defeat.   And all I have now to do is to hit the business of metaphor vs symbol harder than the original did—that, the way it looks now, should be done tomorrow

so i should have it to you a day or two ahead of the iron deadline you gave me when i was in that trouble three weeks ago (the 15th, but absolute, you sd.)

but i am a little puzzled, from your last letter, in which you sd (last week) you were going to the printer the end of the week—that wld have been two days ago!

not that it matters, i dare say, if you already have enough to go to press with.   I should, in any case, like to get rid of this thing. And am glad I had this push to finish it. . . .

OK.   Anxious to hear from you.

CID!

here   't'is

It's not the cleanest copy I have given
you, but I pray I have made all emendations clear enough!

There is only one chore I am putting on
you—AND IT IS A CRUCIAL ONE, particularly in the last narrative,
the Sun Moon gig:
that is, I only had this bad third carbon (it constitutes
this mss, from page 12 on), and as you have in your hand the original, I
hope you will not damn me for asking you to transfer my corrections from
the enclosed pages over to your clean copy ((from page 12 here (page 11
there) on))

I emphasize the changes in the
final narrative, simply because there the changes, small as they are,
shift the style and tone of the whole thing—make it less slangy, and more
formal.   And this, I think is very important.

It was a tough job, as tough a one as I have had to face, simply
because the task attempted is so huge.   And I had hoped to cut down the
opening argument, but I have been over it and over it, and even with the
reordering, and more care, I still can't see that there is any part of it
I can get out without losing some movement essential to the whole.

(I found your letter, by the way,
on it of considerable help, and though I dare say nothing will ever satisfy
another man—nothing ever does me!   i mean, of my own! !—I do hope
I have taken care of the things which balked you, in the original version)

I am also happy, that I met yr
deadline (beat it, I hope, by a day!)
and that all is well. with
♯3 as a whole, and with you
look forward to hear from you

yrs
P.S.
My God, look!   Looking it over for the last time, I did see one huge
cut.   Do me this favor.   Read it as it is and if you are satisfied, FINE.
IF not, then read, enclosed, sealed, NOTE

If the thing is too long—or seems to your fresh eyes—too
argued, what I have just discovered is that there is one fantastic re-
joining: pages 6, 7, 8, 9, 10, &
                 the first half of 11 could
                 be left out
                           (it would be
                 an excision like one of my own eyes!)
                                             but, there is a perfect
jointure from the word "discovery" (bottom p. 5, top p. 6)
over to middle p. 11, starting
                           "I have been living"!

Wild, wild.   And *only* if you think it needs it,
please.
         But god, it knocks me out.
                           Well,
to you, in yr hands

78

CID: . . . As of HU: I figure you were right, to cut clear from the Greeks
to the Maya, and leave out the "arguing"—if tho I do lose that footnote
on "discourse"!

> (As of "commotes", it means, a sweet
> potato, but I'm not sure I have spelled it right—in
> fact, they don't wear shoes, for that matter!   So, the
> whole business there, is a little cockeyed, surrealist,
> let's call it, eh: and not like me, like, they say, eh?
>
> trouble is, "commotes" are a local plant, and so a
> local word, and what the spelling was, of course, we
> couldn't find out from the natives
>   to make it properly
> strange,—if you want to catch it—you might try what
> Con thinks is the spelling:
>   CAYMOTES
>   and if you do,
> shift shoes to SANDALS, eh?

Won't probably make much sense today, because, trying to toss things
a little in the air, to get clear, of the concentrations, which, since I
left Mexico, have had to be too on—not enuf the proper concentrations,
which make verse possible
                       and hungry to be back *away* from argument,
demonstration, or any such things—. . . . .

am anxious to hear from you, how, the Duncan stuff looks—he is probably
surely more like Morse and Bronk than like Creeley and this one, eh?   but
he is a biting lad, and does, as he probably boasted he thought Origin could
stand, have some more *temper*, I think his word is! . . .

    Wish to christ, too, we could get together: so many things piling up—
am somewhat reluctant to leave the lass just now (never know when these
babies are apt to break loose)—but maybe, say, thanksgiving—or winter

in NEW ENGLAND!

                    how abt that?

                        THOUGH, I assure you, IF,   those
birds give me that stake—willy nilly, child or no child—I shall try my best

to get the hell out of here and go where no anxieties breed, where certain temptations are not, where

                        i breathe more

easily

            THIS IS A PART OF THE CRAVING

                      as of what's
ahead
      or what I'd like to see right
now, is
how it is when
the waters are
pink
     for then, surely,
right over our heads, he
would look like the scarab
he is, that is, his
force is downward, the
head over heels man, the arms
nor the legs flying
outwards: not at all
not at all

HELLO

I am aghast, CID, and ask all yr forgiveness.   Damndest thing: here i was
wondering why i hadn't heard from you!   and of course, a cog had slipped
(in the damnable busyness of this fucking place—I hope I warned you,
   that, to get any of my own work done, and at the same time earn my keep,
   crazy lesions happen, so much is in front of me—and i stay, a simple
   man!)
            I had assumed i had written you, i was so full from, yr last letter!

And of course you have not written, because, there, you had given me the
SOLDIERS—and I well know how, such an act, after such an act, one can
only WAIT!
            I beg your pardon as much as I ever begged any man's that
            i should have kept you waiting!   I gash myself.   And will
            send this special, to cover my shame

Damndest thing ever.   So—quietly: PLEASE FORGIVE ME

            Let me go right at the SOLDIERS (and I am wholly sympathetic—the
word is as weak as "sincere", yet, it has, too, the same deepest meaning—
to your problem & intent here, having worked several months in spring
1947 (think it was) on a like material—and had to give it up, for then,
as presenting—*essentially*—the epic mode & material—AND, yet, none
of us KNOW!)

            (((((PS: been very much off, too, the past two weeks—in
                  fact since finishing the rewrite of HU: looking
                  around, for an OUT, not wanting to work, or pre-
                  sent myself to anything.   Yet have.   And yet still,
                  am dreadfully UNHAPPY.)))))

OK, back.   That is, there was something wrong in EP's and then Macleish's
metric, as of, the sort of problem here.   And this is how I would take yr
job, 1st:
         that, the opening couplet, gives the game away!

   that is, *drama,* of earth and men, is, now, a devilish GENERAL(ization)
   (i'd guess the reason is that all things are inflated, and so, even
    such serious study as the one you are here proposing has to be got
    at contrariwise:
                     man as common has to be restored by way of you or
                     me as particular
                                (I emphasize my sympathy, because
I firmly take it that, the reason why you and i (and rob't) are so close,
go along so, together, is that we do respect the common—and who else
does?
         It comes down to a question of *methodology* (and that is as much,
         where verse goes, *metric* as it, surely, is anything else, eh?)

What I like, is, yr idea, to, do it all in, such shorts, following: in
other words, yr *narrative logic* is well taken, but look what happens to
TIME!   it declares itself so sequential, that, a false interest comes in:
just there, you "lose" yr own intent—that, it is not sequence, but
the reiteration (because man is what is going on, is, continuously,
taking it, having it ★ WWII—"You've had it, BO"

((((I hope this is not seeming too—coming in from the general end:
   it is honestly the best way, i am sure, to come at the metric, that,
   1st, I would try to urge you—in such material, in such an area—
   to grab hold, first, (in order to accomplish the common), by
   DOCUMENTATION—the specific

       that is, there are two attacks, possible, on this
       chief of all problems now: A.   *the proper nominative*
         (exact particular specific anecdote explored
         into universe by conjecture—making possible
         all detail, and, essentially, the old logic
         of narrative: PRIME EXAMPLE: Herodotus

or B.   *the erasure of* the proper nominative (but this attack involved al-
    together fresh devices of time, of juxtaposition: in fact, has to be
    solved literally in Non-Euclidean & Geometrical SPACE-TIME ways)

    (the erasure, that is, only of the names, but, a retention of the
     force of the common by not falling for realism, or the false part-
     icularism of the "autobiographical"—that because it happens to
     me, it is therefore, going to be of significance to others::::THIS
     IS THE RANKEST NONSENSE, and one of the things we are fighting,
     through ORIGIN, so thoroughly, that, the MORAL (which all auto-
     biog leaves out, even when it includes it—Gide, e.g., of even Simone
     Weil—all saintness, or revolutionaryisms)
                  THE MORAL IS FORM, &
    nothing else
        and the MORAL ACT is the honest—"sincere" motion
        in the direction of FORM

What happens in THE SOLDIERS, is, that, you fall between these two ways:
by dropping the nominative (except as to place, which, you allow yrself
to fall into—are forced—by the literal historical sequence in time, to
locate), you hope to get a common over all—but, alas, you get a "dissolve"
(literally, in cinematic terms)
                 at the same time, by retaining the
logic of time of the proper nominative, you lose the advantage that
the first act promises you
           (you see, the narrative problem now, in verse
           or prose, involves one first act: a clear &

present DEPARTURE from all thinking in "historical"
frame:
>that is, either (a), that there is truth,
>and that evidence can bring it forth (this
>was what Thucidydes started, and we have
>to put a stop to——it is right here that
>logic and classification most strongly
>work against verse & prose now
>
>or (b), that there is any time except
>that one time which matters, YOUR OWN

(the LIE of history is that a man can find or take any relevance out
of the infinite times of other men except as he pegs the whole thing
on *his* time: and i don't mean times, that sociological lie, I mean
your TEMPI—mine,
>in short, all that TIME IS, is RHYTHYM
(and there is no way of knowing any rhythym OTHER THAN YOUR
OWN, than BY your own

Now if you hold to my use of HERODOTUS, as TONIC, as on which to HOOK
(in order to start thinking in NON-HISTORICAL ways—to start substituting
the art of STORY for the non-art but logic of HISTORY

>(I need not state, here, the other pole, simply
>because your problem, in THE SOLDIERS, is
>obviously just here in this area of distinction
>between history and story

you can begin to make yourself master of materials which (my guess is)
is EXACTLY THE SORT OF MATERIAL WHICH YOU *ARE*—which you are
INTERESTED in—which you will, ahead, BE COMMITTED TO

>you see, there is a sort of "philosophy" aimed at in this
>verse: a position, about man
>>and what i take it is the
>most valuable thing i can give you in critique of it is
>to try to throw light on how you have or have not accomplished
>a *stance* (which is only and always a man's own rythmic position)
>from which to propel such a philosophy

>>(that is, there is truth,
in one sense only, that, you are it if you make yrself clear
>acrostic
>it is the old Latin conundrum, which was tacked on, to
>the Christ-Pontius confrontation:

P: Quid est veritas?

C: Est vir qui adest

And the man who is before you (in this case, you, cid corman) *is* before you (me) to the degree that he projects himself to me by his rhythym

So we come (instead of starting from) the metric (I have no particular quarrel with yr imagery here—or at least think it is eventually con-trolled by this deeper question: that is, the imagery is honestly seeking to be precise, even though it is seeking also to be general or common enough (of earth, sun, mud, heat, breath, feet, etc) to support the "philosophy" of man here presented—of man as soldier:
                earth, air, fire, water—and the 5th element, sd Nap, MUD!

what i think it is important to examine, to get at the whole truth, is the METRIC
                (tenses, also, like the imagery, are a part of the "histori-
                cal" mode—the trap of the "and" in this poem is the
                like problem Perse goes to pieces on (all over the sky
                & sand of Asia, as well, in his other things, the sun
                of the West Indies)
                                but it is—again—an attempt, by
                a certain LARGENESS of tone to reinforce MAN
                                        (my argument
                wld here again be, that any largeness is not extendable
                beyond your own size—which, again, is a matter of,
                YR RYTHYM

So—let's switch to the mss, where, I shall try to analyse, by text, the metrical problem::::::::. . . .

Cid,
        follow one rule *ALWAYS*—take all the time & space you need
        to be precise to what is in your mind or soul to say.   This is
        the true act *of* discourse: the law, say what you have got to say.
        And STOP.   But *SAY* it   so:
                                SONG!

Look: damned bizness, of supper—let me get this off; & we'll take it up from there:

84

You will note that, it is almost exclusively when you
have hewn to the pentameter that I have found flaw
                                    but I would
urge you (as you'd know from PV) to move yrself out away from
any declared base (which becomes a strait jacket) & find only then,
basically, in yrself
                    —and this, I'm sure,
will involve you, 1st, in such *content* questions as,
The Soldiers, also raises and which most of the other
letter is about.   Again, please excuse me wholly for
                    my crazy delay

        the contingent motion of
            each line as it
                moves with—or against—
                    the whole—working
            particularly out of its immediacy.

85

cid:

     yr bad news in, last night (& a previous letter since I wrote you)
and i certainly have no other feelings than, you do what you do, that is,
i so completely respect the rythym with which you have composed issues
1 & 2 that i go along with you, in fact, as you know, it is my opinion
that i never knew another magazine which was as composed as *origin*

     & so long as *round & canon* sit there, a round O, i myself feel
my part in *origin* is advanced, eh?

     i have only one feeling which is this, that, so far as you can
i might hope that one tremendous advantage origin has had to such as
robt & myself may not be lost in the going on of the mag: that—for
the first time for me, at least (& i have noticed that this is a gain
all poets crave: Keats, once, hit this factor in a letter sighing, it
had been a year since he wrote one of the odes and now that it was being published it was of such time back that he had moved on enough to
make the ode's appearance, however he was pleased, of less moment to
him than it might have been)
               —that is, i take it you could depend
upon robt & i to put out at a rate & quality during any three months
to make it possible for you to plan the use of such by six months
from its writing. And of course pretty much such has been the way it
has worked out (example, R & C, written July, appearing Oct 22—or
(*Grace*) or *Party* ?, written August ? appearing same time?)
                    —my worry
is, frankly, that this wonderful business—as i think i have told you, it is,
in itself, *generative*—not be lost. . . .

And there is that matter of Robert Barlow and/or an issue on *SOURCES,*
or ORIGINS: an issue of origin featuring *"origins"*!
                    (That is, as you know,
I favor such "featuring" than "group issue" flatly thinking the Americans
are the ones, now, who are carrying the ball!)
                (Fact is, I am
just about ready myself to do two things: A. an essay (like the PV) on
                              all art centering around,
                              "theater"

        & B. a piece of "mapping" the
whole culture strategy, called something like THE ETYMOLOGY OF ALL THIN

(I will also drop a note now, asking Duncan, where are the mss)

     Ok, for today. Let me hear back on this whole matter.

My dear Cid:
              fullest thanks for all recent notes, gifts & generous
words, as well as the 3rd of my Origin Dollar Series, but i have just
got up out of bed (2:30 AM) to hasten to write you to ask you to give
all yr best attention and act to this rupture of Robert's, simply because i think it is the most important thing imaginable facing you.

   That is, Creeley is a subtle & beautiful man, worth more than all
the rest of us you have published—and then some: your magazine shall
be known in the history of writing because you there first published
the stories and letters of this man.   And that he has, in his present
sickness & despair, heaved off, is something I think you should, so
far as you possibly can, get an ease to.

   You see, Cid, he is a grave and serious man, & his work of an order that causes him to demand back what he gives: utmost care & openness
in discussion of.   On top of that, he has, like any of us to whom the
thing is already our life stretching down to our death, a sense of the
responsibility of the act of writing by anyone anywhere: that sense of
the public domain that only the most serious men ever have, and to which
they give, and sacrifice anything.

   I would urge you to plumb yrself, and give back to this rupture
the very simplest straightest acts you can forge.   There is no tally,
anyhow.   I'm sure Creeley, as I, take it you have given us more than
anyone else who has published us could ever have given us, both in
the welcome you give our work and on top of that the composition in
which you present us in ORIGIN.   That is so much, you need not concern
yrself with anything else, in fact, can well take those two aspects
of attention as of such size no man could offer us more.

                       So do not argue if what else you might
think to give—criticism, of mss, or of problems he or I, say, give
all the attention of our waking & sleeping hours to,—rubs him wrong.
I'd say, learn from him, and in saying it, can tell you that I have
learned more from him than from any living man: he is of that sort of
dimension that you can well allow—and gain thereby—that you do learn,
and modestly learn from him.
                       And this will only increase you.   In other
words, it is not Origin which alone gains, it is yrself.   For he is most
knowing, in the very interstices of sentences, he can breathe and feel out
all that is worth hearing, worth grabbing on to, of another man.

   You will imagine, that if I write to you,—and as seriously as I
do now write—that I do it, not only because you have told me you would
like any considerations I have on the matter, but because I know how

rocked he is, and have written him my strong wish that the three of us, so far as we can, go along together in this venture which already shows so much & can be so much more.

Give it all the quietest, straightest, deepest thing you can.

. . . So these are some days, eh?

p. 53
"To understand realistically and soberly how limited our power is is an essential part of wisdom and of maturity; to worship it is masochistic and self-destructive.   The one is humility, the other self-humiliation."

---

regressive-progressive

---

regressive is
    always to safety
    pre-death state
        (mortality)

---

the need for identity
the wanderer as fugitive

---

the uninhibited
    intelligence
    (child)

RELIGION (from p21—
    Psychoanalysis &
    Religion)

    "any system of thought and
    action shared by a group
    which gives the individual
    a frame of orientation and
    an object of devotion."

BMC
feb 6
52

dear Cid:
            excuse the dilatory domicile—had bad days, without
more cause than the middle of the life, eh?
                                    or the waiting, say,
that san juan de la cruz talks about (i hope!)

                                    am reading, & going
to movies: nothing much more happening, except talk (which grows
less & less usable)....

Keep in touch.   And let me weather this present clam.   (I leave the error)

89

Cid—Base apologies: been in bed two days, but that ain't nothin, mere
recovery—put the screws on, &, in two weeks, put out two long prose
putsches: (I)   HISTORY

> using these States as counters
> & arguing a proper predecession

> > a sort of backhanded salute to
> > Walt Whitman, for his unhappi-
> > nesses

& (II)   CULTURE

> A Wild Stab at its Present Shape etc.

They are whacky, done in "presentation" prose, you know, not written but
thrust—and a pleasure to do.   Now the question is, where to land 'em?
With you planning APPLE for 6, and the selected for 8, I don't figure
you want any more like HU

> (by the way, HU came right in the middle of
> this spung, and was a lifter!

> > just hit it
one afternoon by luck—one has to hope for such a break in seeing one's
own stuff in print, that, one can catch oneself off guard, and read it
fresh—and it worked: my, how much i was inside it, inside it as i hadn't
been even in the writing, for, then, it was day in & out, & even the rewrite, but this time—one sweep, and i had it: very damned rewarding,
and glad you put it out, glad, too, that you made that cut—think it
rolls as is, and is much more its own organism than that Malinowsky
quote wld have allowed. . . .

Of course, still, for this citizen, it's THE REPLY TO GERHARDT which
woofs.   I don't know why, on this one, I am its only champion (even you
say, HU is the "best" thing in ♯4!) HU may be the text but the DEMON-
STRANDUM is also right there!

. . . OK.   Keep me on on all matters.   And don't mind if I disappear once in
a while: I miss my Washington isolation & routine, that method of mine of
going ahead for days, day after d, without interruption, bearing down.   And
to do it here means several rigidities: even have to make myself damned
unpopular by refusing to carry my lift of the stick (washing dishes, attending
lunch, cutting wood, doing the chores as a member of the board of fellows etc.
—I figure if I get to the faculty meetings on Friday nights, and shove it out
the two nights I work for 'em (Monday & Thursday, and I assure you I work—
5 hrs at a clip, each of those nights.   So when a necessity takes me, as that
one, two weeks ago, I have to exclude so much.

> > Will see you see both
of the go's as soon as I can figure out where to send them, and make

copies:
>they are full of social (economic) & political (cultural)
>examples, laws, & punctuations
>>(more like ISH & G&C than
>>HU, or, PV)

. . . Write, & keep writing even if i lag—for i am going to will some
verse into existence (I hope!) any day now (he sd, the god-tempter!)

Cid: Many thanks for all news—and you are right, I have trouble getting
TIME, especially when i have been as bloody damn sick as i have been for
the past three weeks (don't know what it is—showed up as a boil in the right
armpit, crippling me—had that lanced, and penicillin shot in my arse,
600,000 units, but i remain daily below par: probably the Bear, & Winter,
and Spring too far be—Hind!)

Am busy, at the moment, at my old last, Mr Melville: accepted to do a
review of two new books, one his, one on him, for the *New Republic;* and
it involves much labor, in that both are put out by those creatures, the
academics (all three of whom—2 edit MD, a centennial edition, with 250
pages of annotations!   I have known in the past: Vincent at Ill Tech, Mansfield
at Williams, and Thompson (who writes *this* book—M'S QUARREL WITH
GOD, by god!)   who went to school with me & is now—if it is the same guy—
Prof at Princeton

> i am tempted, instead of what i took the review for: to have another
> go at saying my piece abt MD—to lace em good by writing SOME
> PRINCIPLES FOR CORRECT EDITING OF H M!

> for at least V & M have put out a pretentious & ill-proportioned
> edition—and left all but one important thing unsaid (they do
> add a tremendous quotation from Goethe to the Melville record—
> on daimonism—beautiful thinking by G: 1st time he ever struck
> his way into me—and the observation is crucial behind HM's
> management of Ahab, in fact, behind his whole advance on the
> problem of heroism, than which no one (Goethe, Carlyle, Emerson,
> Nietsche, Freud) touched him

I took great offense at yr German translator's doggerel (isn't he the same
man you quoted me a year ago, on my work in ♯1?

He strikes me as another
of those Europeans (like my once-friend Giorgio di Santillana, now Prof at
MIT) who is bright enough, but who never found a keel for their cut-water
in themselves, and thus are left with no element, and stand silly in mid-
air slashing around with a brain which has nothing to saw on

> i wld send all such to, say, HOLDERLIN, to his suffering, to
> cause them to shut their mouths—or stop their stupid shining
> sword, unflashing

> > or to Klee, with his *superb intellect* (the proper
> > use of same)

> > or to DHL, who—directly—tells
> > any such that the 4th temptation,
> > left out of the parable, is the

intellect, trying to go it, alone:

it always ends up high & dry with knowledge or history or schemes for its own eating—eating itself

And my anger is—the anger of all men who write from their own suffering, that, you can't put us down with *schemas*—you can't wag yr fingers—yr weak cocks—in our faces: we do what we are obliged to do: measure us by what you have done with what you've had to do with, brother: we say that to them. And if they once faced that, dealt with that, instead of what their light heads take off our work (like peeling our skin) they'd stop such shit—and find out, that HOW A THING IS SAID is as important as WHAT IS SAID, that *it is* WHAT IS SAID

93

CID; *that* raises me!   EVERY TWO MONTHS—fine, beautiful, faster.   Ok

But JOURNAL—what, exactly, is that format?   Sounds lighter, less
aesthetic, more pressing, fresher.   Could be a light guerilla wagon, for
shooting across the heavy public press & publishing (such as ANNUALS,
TWICE A YEARS, and all such deadness)

YET: I am immediately nervous by your analogies and your decisions,
and want very precisely to ask you to examine the very premises of those
two wonderful aspects of the change: SPEED, and LIGHTNESS.   For why do
you liken yrself to NYtimes, HT, SAT rev, or whatever?
                                                    why do you speak
of "reviews"—and unsigned reviews?
                                   and why do you say APOLLONIUS is
out, when you also say the 16 pp is the equal of 64, and are the man who
used a whole no. of a quarterly to issue a 64 page essay on Stevens?

> (question #1: i should like to know, in the
> light of what you say abt APOLLONIUS, what
> you intend to do with the other "play" you
> were to use in #6, Mr Williams' DESERT
> MUSIC?))

Now I want you to know that anything i say here has only to do with myself and my own work on the most serious of grounds—that is, I rather
think you know that publication of anything of mine is *not* my ambition,
that my ambition is only making more work—and so, for me, any such
publication as you have given me as no one else ever did is all so fine
an experience, so damned beautiful a thing, that I do not thank you, I
love you.
          So, when one is that "free", it doesn't matter to me if you
never publish another thing: you not only have published me fulsome-
ly, but also, I should not deserve to have been published as you did
publish me—to have you call me, in CONTACT, the center of yr
push (was it?)—if I were not wholly independent.
                                                And so, what you do
do at every step of yr way, is crucial to me: I can enjoy being published
by you so long as I think you are going in a forward direction.   I want
you to do that.   For I want to stay with you.

OK.   Back to what I take to be the gains of SPEED, and LIGHTNESS.   How
can one edit, and keep these qualities in the material published?
((Please, at this time, refer to that long go I wrote you a year and
a half ago, when ORIGIN was still in a like stage—when I tried to
get down to you a principle of what I might now call *interaction of
planes of expression*:
                      and let me, now, suggest anew some of the implica-

tions, as well as in the light of yr editing of ORIGIN through ♯5

You say (in this letter before me) "I believe if this new mode of presentation is handled with as much freshness and alertness to possibilities that it can be much more effective as an organ for new writing
here and abroad".
                    You see, this, to me, is the nub of it: (1) alertness
to possibilities (what other possibilities are there, today, except the
tremendous interaction of fields, so tremendous that the day is just
ahead when the scientist will be again solely the artist, simply, that
the scientist himself has found that the one mystery left is form, and
the morphology of same

and (2) "new writing, here and abroad" (what kind? "creative writing"?
that is mere aestheticism, wherever it is, and you yrself carry, on
yr masthead—and damn well mean, I knowing you—not that but writing
and reading "for the creative"—
                    which is a wholly different thing (it is
NOT the Beloit Poetry Journal, and all that goes with it—not one of
those people, and if you publish anyone of them (exception Wilbur, but
GOD HELP US *not* such two verses as he was unconscionable enough to
allow to be published there) wholly different thing than such "culture"—
cultch or culch, meaning (literally, look it up) RUBBISH

You see, Cid, this is a *hard* trade, hard, simply, that expression is
itself hard work and the place from which it comes—a life—is a
hard thing (there is no softness allowable in anywhere, especially
in one self—and I mean that for myself as well as for you)

Let me repeat my deepest nervousness about "writing abroad", as an
editing principle (you will recall I heaved off on this from the start,
and feel so that ♯4 was not CLEAR, simply, that that problem is
a deep one—and please, please, GO EASY with this guy
you call yr co-translator
                    (look, the trade is also lonely: I know
what it is to have a friend, but believe me—in your business—you
have (I honestly, seriously think)—in your editing of this new
venture as well as in ORIGIN—you have two friends, simply because
they are serious men, with all that means—and I mean, means:
Creeley, and Olson
                    (they are, and if you give them such an opportunity
                    as 16 pages each two months, you can get out of them
                    poems, stories, plays AND CRITIQUE PLUS OTHER
                    WRITERS—

christ, i can see Creeley, right now, pouring M. Elath at you as a guy
to catch (like I did Barlow—he had not, then, committed suicide; Perkoff—
he had not then fell back before critique—and Perchik—did he ever send

you anything?)

        and i would—or do now—pour Elath at you. For I stumbled on him, accidently, myself, in INTRO independently of Bob, and now that you offer such a new fresh venture, I'm telling you: GET ELATH, and even look over this editor, Brigante

in fact, look over INTRO

        (and don't, please, think that the new ORIGIN can't be ahead of anything:
        it all depends on the care of your own thinking. But please, Cid, do take stock—and I don't mean on moneys, etc. On that side, I have full respect for you, that you did it—YOU DID IT— you put that damned thing out, got it out, for 5 issues. Gave me that ride. WOW. Think of it, as ACCOMPLISHMENT. but also, think of this other thing: EDITING. It takes absolute hardness—and a series of the most essential recognitions.

        Look: I so believe in the possibilities I will answer every letter you send me on it on receipt. But please: the way we can participate—the way I can—is if you will tell me, detail by detail, how your thinking goes. And if you will stay open to all my own thinking in the same area.

You see, I know it is hard to take any other man's conceptions, but believe me, I offer anything not as Olsonisms, not at all (be sure of that) but as what is necessary
        that i had to learn
           and am learning
               but that i have
put a lot into

    (1)   the kinetics of things—and so know how a magazine can be composed kinetically

    (2)   the present state of knowledge—and so how a magazine can disclose that state

    (3)   the exactitude of a work of art—and so how a mag can go by taste, and be not aesthetic

  &(4)   the lie of a wide audience—and so how a mag must live by the will of clear men, and not trade, for an instant, with the theory that audiences make magazines

        (question #2: have you yrself read, or do you think there was ever many readers for THE LITTLE REVIEW, THE DIAL, or the early POETRY (look what happened to that

96

thing when the audience widened—did the
great poets arise?   or did they damn well
betake themselves off from that area, and
leave the thing to secondraters, and imi-
tators?)

I'm for you, but please, let's get going fresh, fierce, and openly—I'll
write any issue of 16 pages myself, anytime!

This is only a jab, to move
us forward—very excited,
by the change

cid:

what you forget is, any of us asks (expects) more from the thing
or person closest to us—or at least, it matters more what movement forward there is, in what is close (whatever one puts on anyone or thing
out there, what dream, if it isn't in the end, that thing, it is no where
near as devastating as—the world isn't or if it goes up in a puff tomorrow
—as you or Origin is, to me, say

so don't for a moment think I put you or Origin in any one-one
comparisons—that is, other than Origin-Origin!   All I shall forever ask
is that your own pages put any single page of any other mag to shame!   That,
surely, is the measure—and no more

and just because, for me, Origin is "my place", you will please
enjoy my concern—take all critique as that sort of constant nagging we
give to those we love, simply, that we want 'em perfect.   Or what is
heaven for.

e.g., on Bjerknes, i would imagine (from my small reading of
him) that you are probably right to keep asking more of him, &
yet (to suport such demand) you must be careful not to publish a single
page which is not *better* than he.

(Ok.   These are simplicities—and like
all such, come across polyanna to the person who hears them from another.
Just because one does say them to oneself—that's why they irritate.
The trouble is, it is so very hard to act simply.)

Please keep me on, on all developments.   For there are signs
that Origin has already been that spur a good little mag is.   (I wouldn't
myself, read Laughlin's Folly as any such danger.   Au contraire.   It is
going to be such a Main Line shit as all such several recently are—all
the New Nationalism (like the 15 American Painters show, in NY, this spring,
and like all Ciardi adventures:
more sign that the Right and the Left are
synonymous, now (Chicago and New York are become as filthy, in literary
and cultural affairs as Washington financially and politically: I don't
know that I have ever sufficiently said to you that ORIGIN, simply that
it is from a three-decker in Dorchester, is implicitly RIGHT, and CLEAR:
Boston.   (I have even, to friends, said that it presages a proper cultural revolution: ORIGIN, BOSTON (even the rime, and the name of it, is
pure)
my cry is, the beloved thing, make it, perfect.   And what I would
only, solely, constantly, urge on you is, yourself: make yourself in the
image of—yr mag.   (Not vice versa, for, tho that sounds logical, it
is only lyrical: I have deeply found that work leads one on, not, one

leads one's work on.   So you, there:

$$\text{that is, you have published}$$

(a) *critique* which goes to the heart of the present problem in
         (1) the kinesis of culture
         (2) prose, & narrative, now—Bob on prose, perhaps me
                              on THE ESCAPED COCK
      &(3) "art" now—Bob, in his letters, say

(((you will note i do not include Morse on Stevens, and the reason—dear friend—
    is not any difference from Stevens—it is never that easy—but the degree
    of apprehension of the reality contemporary to us.   For that reality, at any
    time, is demonstrably there, and demonstrably is *properly* engaged (this
    any of us comes to find out not by any eclecticism, but by that act I make
    so much of, *recognition*.   And recognition rests solely on the work—the
    amount of price paid by you, or me.
                              Also.   Stevens is a profound misleader
simply that he is in a deeply important area (what I have yet no better word
for than *ornamentation*:
                    this is of such importance—and tho it lies implicit
in Gate and Center, it is still something I should wish to explore more
completely in a piece for you.   (I did a job on painting here a couple of
weeks ago which was again the kick.   But I was not satisfied with it.   In
fact I would still say none of us are that far along that we can say
(((we might *do*))) what it is
IN COLD HELL, was my try

> It is that deep, that it is a wholly different
> disposal of attention to *anything*.

> It is what all the cry of myth & rite is
> falsely about

> It is how men take life (collectivism is
> another of its signs)

> Yet it shall come to be in its own guise—
> and modern man is altogether too literate
> yet (in his thinking, in his trying to push
> it into existence, like as tho he were capa-
> ble of couvade!

You see, the problem is to clear ourselves of the negatives—all Greek
myth as we distribute our attention to it *after* Herodotus, as well as
such men of decoration as Stevens

> (example, is Matisse as important as
> Cy Twombly will be—is, already, for
> those of us who have had the chance to
> see his stuff

(The fact that you don't know Twombly is—directly—my fault.   But it

is one of those lesions of attention that would not happen if you were
constantly stuck with open space in Origin simply because you were not
convinced that Morse or that gas station owner or any of those European
poets deserved your space

((now, right here, don't, please, Cid, think
that you need to defend yourself.   Do you think I think it is easy to get to
the point where one is leaving white space white simply, that what one
would fill it with, is not fit for it?   I damn well don't, and, from that little
spurt this year which died out—to do those Broadsides—I damn well learned
what a trap editing is, how many forces of practical reality one is involved
in, instantly.

My point is otherwise: that you are moving in that direction.
And the irony is, that if one is not so moving, one is falling back—one is
quickly behaving "like others"!

Forgive me if I spell this out a little
(and please, my touchy friend—and you are, you know, and this is as much
a sign of your life—I am, too: one is forced to back up on what one does do
because one damn well knows it ain't anything compared to what one dreams
of doing ((((this is another face of my point at the beginning of this letter))))

but (1) as of European poets—or "foreign":

I honestly don't think
(and I finally don't think you don't think likewise) *any*
contemporary—or "new" poets—outside the Americans are
capable of the pushes the Americans are
So: if you were taking the clue from yr own masthead—that
epigraph—the "foreign" or "European" or "Asiatic" poets you would be
publishing
      SUMERIAN
        AMERICAN INDIAN
          MAYAN
            CHINESE
              EGYPTIAN
                ARCHAIC GREEK   etc   etc

(You see, I don't believe that a little mag today is serving its function
if it takes for granted the proposition which was important in the '10s
and '20s—when the Americans did need a place to make their heave
public—that NEW writing and INTERNATIONAL culture were called for
------ you will agree, I think, that both of these "planks" are still
the dominant ones of the leetle mags

Now one reason why yr fellow editors are fearful of Laughlin's HINDSIGHT,
USA (that latest of the MARSHALL PLANS, and like those, "international"
as the US EMPIRE is necessarily world-wide (Persian oil, Indonesian rubber,
and the danger from the real masses—the Chinese, Indian, and East Russian)
is precisely that Hutchins Etc (State Dept and Publishers) have swallowed

up their premise
                    (just listen to those pitiful voices, . . . any of em—
                    or the Left, to their anarchist-aesthetic Right)

          ORIGIN—the very name you gave it: look, it is implicitly new, not
          because it introduces new names (it does that, surely, Creeley, Olson!)
          but because it introduces—or should—new premises of experience

one thing right off the bat which makes ELATH fresh, is, that he is already
far enough along to know that the old necessary quarrel with science is
passe—that he knows, spang, that *methodology* has displaced "technique",
that Korsibski is more use to a writer than any of his fellow writers, etc.

     (I have no right to ask that you initiate all things—in fact, which
     one of us does?   i was struck, for ex., in proofing APOLLONIUS
     for you, to see i had used that image of violets, springing up on
     all sides, in the spring—as of men, when the time is right

     all, finally,. i am saying is, lean on yrself (who had the instinct to
     create this magazine, in the first place, to give it that title, that
     epigraph, to be open enough to publish Creeley, Olson, Perkoff,
     that one fine poem of Wilbur's, to do that fresh thing, edit in those
     personal letters)—and lean on your writers, not all of them, but
     those who are dedicated not to publishing—to getting themselves
     published—but to their work, and that only because they are dedicated
     to their lives
                    (I'm sure you can smell any writer who sends you stuff
                    merely to cultivate yr acquaintance in order to acquire
                    your pages!

                    ((one reason why i suspect any too great a connection on
                    your part with any other little mag is, that I know myself
                    that such reading deflects one's primary attentions

                    in fact, i can go further, and say that any too much
                    reading of mss. coming in is dangerous, simply, that
                    any of us admire good writing, and want to publish it—
                    it is a pleasure to see any man arise above his permanent
                    incoherence)

Make a demand of, say, Creeley and myself—not just for our own stuff,
but for any other material we think right

     I, for example, am constantly, in reading, coming on those sorts
     of documentation which I mentioned to you in that original letter
     a yr and a half ago:

               when i sd Barlow, and reprinting Sauer, say

     right now, for example, I'd say, reprint the first five pages of

Saturday

Cid: writing the above so stimulated me, that I launched, and maintained,
a five hour go on a backporch all yesterday afternoon! It pivoted around
a girl who was born a Sirokin in Boston, raised in Van Cortland Park, and
is now the wife of Billings, the Work director here, and wood worker. She
is of the protest class, who harks back rightly to what her parents were (are
(Odessa) as against what she finds most of her contemporaries. And what
I was faced with—with her, her husband, a Lafarge, and the daughter of
Ohio middle class wealth!—was, exposing the nature of these States to
their understanding, their joint understanding.

It was fascinatingly diffi-
cult—as is the reality bearing on us, what?

the approximate identity of
the Right and the Left, that—"Conspiracy": how to see how
one system basing itself on credit and so limiting production
in the face of its own technological forward motion comes more
and more to resemble and collaborate (essentially) with another
system, basing itself on an unobservable destitution of the
masses, which consolidates all power in a political leadership
and ends up expanding only those productions which enable it
to oppose the other system in war—and so each comes, by the
final act of itself, more to resemble the other than any common
difference of the citizens of each

It is not my kick, as a post-modern and so a post-Darwinian, yet I grapple
again and again with these terms, to see. What the session did, though,
was to reemphasize for me the conviction that the only morality is art,
and that this has been becomes now so crucial that one can be sure that
art as a principle is once more back in business as the only essential
"revolution"—that only as men are bred to think of expression as the
only social act worth any interchange with another human being is there
anything ahead but more of same, and that it is exactly in this sense
that Hawkes (in that passage) lays bare the tremendous change of man
which took place sometime in the Pleistocene, when he abandoned evolution
as the arising of his species (stopped with his opposable thumb) and
substituted culture for evolution—decided that he wanted most to make
things and then, instead of showing his son by example, he invented language
to show him and succeeding generations by precept. Only in this fact as
faith is individuality restored—individuality, and particulars. And is
class as an ambience cut through—with all its attendant obfuscations.
I believe, for example, that all men and women can dance—and this
alone is enough to establish expression—that all other expression is only
up from this base; and that to dance is enough to make a whole day have
glory, granting that work is called for of each of us. The hook is that
work will always make sense if dancing is understood to be—expression is—
the other issue of a day.

"Our class"—the non-class—the a-class—the

expressers solely, now have the responsibility to restore expression to
such prime place.   (I take it you understand yr own masthead—for the
creative—to be this distributable—that all men and women are "creative"
in this sense, that they are capable of "expressing" themselves.

And it is

the only answer to the spectatorism which both capitalism and communism
breed—breed it as surely as absentee ownership (whether of a leisure class
or of a dictatorship, in the "proletarian" sense) doth breed it, separating men
from action as surely as—as a leadership—these two identities limit
production, or regulate it, in that monstrous phrase which turns all
things toward creation's opposite, destruction.

For to be a spectator is

to assert an ownership in it which is absentee—a movie, or a painting,
or a poem (and the corrolary is, of course, the actual ownership, by
the vested interests, of those more permanent acts of expression which
we call "the arts".

        (You can not own a poem until you use it—and
        there is only one way you can use a poem: it invokes
        if it is a proper act of expression only its like,
        that is, expression, no matter how that expression
        may be different from a poem.   Certainly no poet
        wants any hearer to write a poem—he don't essen-
        tially, believe any other can equal his.   (In
this sense I understand Blake's proposition that, for a poet, there
can be no other.   This is true, not relative—and has to be dealt
with as a permanent, not a qualifying, fact—as an absolute, in
this sense in which Pierre Boulez (to whom I have inscribed IN COLD
HELL) specifically says music is now capable of being absolute:

    "serial structure of notes (the twelve-tone scale, and post-
    same) tends to destroy the horizontal-vertical dualism, for
    'composing' amounts to arranging sound phenomena along 2
    coordinates: duration and pitch.   We are thus freed from
    all melody, all harmony and all counterpoint, since serial
    structure has caused all these (essentially modal and tonal)
    notions to disappear".

((A propos art and technology:

        techne as root means "an art"   !   adj.
                and *technic/*
        (meaning ♯ 3 reads: *Stock Exchange.*   Designating,
        or pert. to, a market in which prices are
        mainly determined by manipulation or
        speculative conditions.   !
  technics,   n., reads:
        "The doctrine of arts in general; branches of
        learning relating to the arts"

and (to round off these incredible cross-shoots) *technology* is literally
the science of the arts

My interest in this is from a sense that, say, in
verse, the technique is now something we must expect, is not, as it was
such a short time ago, a counter to use as a stick to get the practice cleaned
up—"verse should be at least as well written as prose"—cannot be given
the special respect any more than technology can, in our society, or it
will run straight ahead into super-science as organization of man—that
form must be carefully extricated from these mechanicals (however essential
they are)—just as carefully as Boulez is after form in serial *structure*:

form, "the shape and structure of anything".

Yet we stay faced with the
necessity for a word to cover the process by which form is accomplished
to the degree that it is deeper than technique—to the degree that
there is a will to form, an initiation in us to express "forms", to bring
them into being.
(It is a curious light the Greek equivalent—morphe—
throws, in this aspect as root to that god Morpheus
—which needs to be repossessed, by the way—to be
cleared of Miltonic and Romantic special use—
"the fashioner", because of the shapes he calls up
before the sleeper.
Nota: you will know, of course,
how much I take dream to be such a sign of that confusion out of which all but the highest art emerges:
I put it that way—so condition it—because I am led to think that
there is a stage where man is free of dream. And that that stage is where
he is utterly clear, limpid, in this sense that he has so possessed his
own "form", so knows the structure of himself (in the face of all other
forms) that he works from that alone. This, it would seem, is about
the only excusable way in which the word genius might be used. And
this use seems, again, to be root-right: fr the verb, to beget. Certainly,
finally, if a man could so "free" himself into himself as to be bothered
by no unconscious shape—to be as much master of that as we take it we
are of conscious shape—then, and only then, can he be called a begetter.
For that act—the act of birth—is the most exclusive one, that, whatever
the contributary causes (conception, "to take in", or procreation—which
does still carry the force of before creation) in the issue the act is *one*
person's, the actual begetting, the physical fact.)

And the word which seems to me of as much moment as all the concept of
"the full bearing" which plays so much a part in my work (and which
I believe Elath means when he speaks of "totality") is the word I use

and use and am not sure of the place and play of: METHODOLOGY.   For,
like morphology, this tendency of the present to admit the "-logy"
in is highly significant
                              (it is again the same as above, that, the
    principle of art is now as crucial as the works of art—that
we shall not again have a habit of art (persons shall not know
    how crucial expression is, for their lives) until we make abundantly
    clear how art *is* a principle
                              (((Nota, editor of: "A source or ORIGIN;
                                   primordial substance; ultimate basis
                                   or cause"))

Methodology keeps forcing itself into my mouth as the word to cover
the necessities that the execution of form involves.   And I shall
again, right now, to see what light I can throw on it, etymologically.

Take it flatly:
                    The science of method or arrangement; hence:
                    (a) A branch of logic dealing with principles of
                          procedure
                    (b) *Educ.*   The science which describes and evaluates
                          arrangements of materials of instruction

   Now that makes this sense (in the light of my own usage of the word)
that it insists logically upon principles of procedure and, educationally,
on arrangements of materials
                          and this is efficient, if you think of the
double problem (which I take as one) of the person himself and any given
form he makes—that any of us is efficient to the degree that we do
get down to principles of procedure—(I do not know that this secondary
stage is arrivable at without the prior discovery that principle itself
matters!)—and that we do see ourselves or any given thing as materials
to be arranged
                          That is, you will note i am lending methodology, already,
kinetic aspects (as it has been used it is drily a function of logic and
knowledge as history).   And I do that because of prior concepts of COHER-
ENCE (you will recall the push I tried to give this concept in G&C—
as against the will to disperse—or, now, I would more oppose the will
to limit, as a false form of the will to cohere, believing, deeply, that
the act of the present (on the part of a man of art) is to capture, from
the enemy, the very forces which make them the leadership, viz:

    organization, the principle of

        efficiency, the characteristic of the machine (on which they
        ultimately base their rulership of us, not, notice, on us,
        or on their own efficiency)

        and *quantity*, the factor of (that increase, of people,

resources, and—and this is not enough noticed—of
sighting—the world, for example, as a "view" now
so automatic (and i am distinguishing it from
the "international", that inaccuracy, or at least that
"national" way of putting it; and emphasizing how
the "world" as a "one"—in the deepest sense—knocks
all sanctions which rested on the local—the self-
contained unit of farm, barter, cooperative, or "natural
rights" etc., into a cocked hat

In other words, to turn the totalitarian—to expose it—by going below
it to see that it rests on a series of altogether new intellectual premises,
more, total premises and behaviours which the word TOTALITY (understand me, not as a descriptive phrase, but as a recognition of the
dominant kinetic which informs the reality we are a part of) does indicate.

To cohere means to stick together!   To hold fast, as parts of the same
mass!
      And coherence is defined as connection or *congruity* arising from
      some common *principle* or idea

Now if I slug in juxtaposition and composition by field, METHODOLOGY
as a word of more import than technique—as a word also as proper to
the change of procedure demanded of us in the face of TOTALITY—may
be more of the cluster of force i take it it is.

But let's go back to root: to *methodos*, and look!
                           with a way,
        with a via, with a path (weg, that which died, and does
not die, which it is any man's job—and the more so now, when the old
way is dead, long live the methodology
                         in other words, the science of
the path—what could be more exactly what we are involved in—it is
not the path, but it is the way the path is discovered!
                  Q E D

Or even current usage, definition 2:
                        orderly arrangement, elucidation,
      development, or classification, more generally, *orderliness*
    and *regularity* or *habitual practice of them in action*!

You see, Cid, I am more and more persuaded that the revolution I am
responsible for is this one, of the identity of a person and his
expression (that these are not separable)—and that this is why
art is the only morality
               yet, saying that, is nothing compared to
getting to grips with how that identity is now accomplished

               and what I have suggested herein

is that (1)   TOTALITY is the character of reality now
    &(2)   that METHODOLOGY is the discipline to master it

and the totality of a person, and his expression, is the degree of
his act of
            organization, efficiency (obviously, this way, human)
            and quantity (in the sense of how much he manages to include
            ——and that he has to include one hell of a lot)

and the methodology is
            (1)   to have a path
            (2)   and that such a path is only accomplishable
                  by the habitual practice of orderliness
                  and regularity *in action*

Ok.   I must quit.   Ravenously hungry (tell yr mother I think often of that
superb meal she served me)

                  This went in several directions, but you
may be able to find it of some use in yr present troubles over the
continuance of the life of this organism which you begot—this
thing I love,   ORIGIN.

                  See you

cid—
     taking a break / maybe for good, i dunno /
wish it might, but will see

     point of this card is: wld you ask A.
Fang, when you see him, if Mathews Chinese-Eng
Dictionary (rev. Am. ed, Harvard '44) is the
best one for a gringo,
                  how much it costs,
                        & if
he knows a way of paying minimum for it—that
is, by discount, or maybe 2nd hand around those
parts
     much obliged

         And let me hear fr you

THE POEMS   THE PROSE
    of   of
   C. O.   THE TRANSPOSITIONS   C. O.
                of
                C. O.

Cid:
      such wld be, for me at this moment, three books i shld like to have
you issue—that is, i put them out to you that way as ends of arcs in case
you do continue to exist as publisher for the term after ♯8

            THE POEMS would be—will be—ready
for you in October, and my present desire is to make them very complete: to
have as many as possible in those 64 pages—wld favor small point type, &
wide page, so that the full impact of them both in line and in number may
be there (after all, it is time somewhere anyone might be able to buy all
that I have done in verse.   And I care for cleanness, and sharpness, of
publication, not doo-daddling

            THE PROSE is such things as the pieces like
G & C, and HU, and PV (plus, i shld think, maybe switching THE STORY
of a O, over into this book rather than in the verse)—and several unfinished
pieces in mss.   which (due to this year plus a wavering of my aims) i have
not wrapped up.   But will, I'd guess, soon (now that I am back at my last).

            THE TRANSPOSITIONS are the
least known and the least done, but they are a project I have been at
now for years (they are, chiefly, from the Mayan glyphs and from the
Sumerian).   In fact, I wld open them with LA CHUTE, perhaps—pulling it
(like the Story of O) over from the poems proper.
                (Such a volume wld be
a chance to establish a body of discipline from stone & clay which wld,
for my taste, be of more use than translations from the Provencal or
the Japanese.
      It wld, in fact, be chips from the wood I work most for my
own proper verse.)

        Anyhow, this to keep you, to let you know I am back
here (I missed Kate and Con, and it was costing me more than I could afford).
But in any case, for the next months, i shall be back & forth, until the
economics declares itself one way or the other. . . .

             Good luck in all matters,
and the fondest regards of C. O.

Wash   Wed   Sept 24

Cid:
      Not to answer yr letter direct to me yesterday, but to get back
to you the enclosed Schwartz, which came in fr BMC in the morning mail

      I don't think I'll bother with him, in fact, I'd have to see the
Hedley to do it—cld you spare yr copy for a few days, to me, here?. . .

      Yet I am immensely grateful to have you keep calling such things
to my attention.   It is like going out for an evening to anybody's house—
the take you get of yr human contemporaries, and the state of same!
What such does is invoke me.   Never direct, but such stimulate and make
taut my own feelings and thoughts, and stuff issues (exs., that I did not
write a letter to the Gloucester Summer Sun, but I, MAX, 3—and HU,
as you may recall, issued fr my horror of ND XII—was, in fact, started
almost like a review. . . .

      You see, it is so silly to engage Schwartz, or Hedley, for me,
having on the record, Winter, 1945-6, THIS IS YEATS SPEAKING, in
Partisan Review, on the Pound Case (and not, notice, any such late
biz as the Bolingen, but, the INDICTMENT, THE TREASON, the
BIZ)
      on top of that, as you'd know, in the Creeley correspondence, there
is a steady spate of examination by me of E.P.'s *limits*, not this lazy
biz, "great poetry" but o, such miserable politics.   But how great is the
verse, and what value is there in the politics.   And the major thing, the
mytho-culture measure of him (what these little lib-labs and seedy young
men of good will don't even guess is the demand to be put upon him, you,
me, them, any body these flat times

                    Wash
                  Fri
                Nov 7

Cid—
        . . . All's well.   I am sorry to have been so silent.   But it is one
of those times when one is in a necessity which involves such a con-
centration one leaves off all other intercourse . . .

How are you?   and what is the latest literary news?   (I feel as far away
as though I were in Hudson Bay or Sitka, and wintered-in.   Yet I rise,
too, to the thought of work ahead, once I have come into possession of
my self again.   (I spent so much, Black Mt.).   In fact begin to really
chew & savor getting that volume ready for you.

        OK—to be on, this one day at least.

                                And fondest regards & hopes
                                you yrself are
                                moving

111

Cid—

What I am in is something only I could get into.   It is not a
crisis.   It is one of those central crucial engagements some men
do, I suppose, walk up to (in the dark, &, I guess, in the middle
of life)

Anyhow, it is wholly exclusive, & excluding—allows nothing
in but itself.

And for the 1st time in my life I am finding out what it is to have
a wife, and friends.

You are my friend: you have given me the *only* continuous
audience I have ever had.

Now: .two days ago I had sat down to write you to tell you my
present state is so essentially where my verse came from that to
look at any of it done previously was literally unbearable––traumatic,
say.   And so to beg back not only that Jan. 1st deadline, but also to
tell you that, if I could do it at all, it might be at an impossible––even
dangerous––cost.

Now this may be present—& in a thing like this, time can swell
& break in an instant.   But my hunch is, knowing the scholar I am,
that I won't let any of this go (and it is my very whole life back to
backwards) until it's exhausted.

Instead of writing you, again "The Mother" in my present vinegar
swelled, and I was taken over: Result, due to delay: two letters in from
Creeley (1st I've heard), announcing Roebuck Press, promising Olson
MAYAN LETTERS (a terrific *gift* to me just now!), and asking to do
the *Origin Poems*—100 bucks, he says!

My present situation leads me to go him
one further––or (depending on your decision between Sankey & Creeley)
a counter-offer: in any case, that the job will be sure to be *edited*, at
least, if he, as another friend, will be my stand-in, in this emergency.
I have written to ask him.

Will you, therefore, Cid:

(1) accept Robt to do my part of the job—select the poems, type, pages, etc?
&(2) consider even more, in the light of (1), the possibility of having them,
there, do the volume?

It will be the finest thing I can hope for at this juncture if the two of
you can come to the best agreement, and thus insure that my present
situation doesn't cause me to fumble, do wrongly, or lose this publication
I have set my heart on––& have profoundly thanked you, inside myself,
for making possible. . . .

Anyhow, as I say, this thing I am in the grip of leaves me of no use to
anyone, not even my wife & child.   So believe me, Cid, all you can do to
get our job done thru R.C. will be the very biggest help to me in my need.

1st working plan for: Dec 4-5, 1952

IN COLD HELL, IN THICKET

poems

Charles   Olson

Origin

Boston, 1953

_____

in lower right corner of right page opp. copyright back of title-p

> yr eyes, yr naiad
> arms

_____

next right page to carry a large numeral "I", and *on the same page,*

LA PREFACE

_____

the book proper to open on the 3rd right page, to be marked page 1, with

THE KINGFISHERS

and the following poems to follow in normal order and to make up
section I:
       ABC's 1, 2, 3
       THERE WAS A YOUTH WHOSE NAME WAS THOMAS GRANGER
       SIENA, 1948
       OTHER THAN
       AT YORKTOWN
       THE PRAISES
_____

next right pages after Section I, to carry a large numeral "II", and,
on same page,

LA CHUTE

_____

Section II to open with IN COLD HELL, and to be followed by:
                 MOVE OVER

A ROUND & CANON
THE MOON IS THE NO. 18
THE TOWER (La Torre)
FOR SAPPHO, BACK
THE RING OF
AN ODE ON NATIVITY

————————————

next right page after Section II, to carry a large numeral "III", and,
on same page,

THE LEADER (in shortened, sharpened, revised version)

————————————

Section III to open with THE GERHARDT

    and to be followed by A PO-SY, A PO-SY
                                   A DISCRETE GLOSS
                                   CONCERNING EXAGGERATION
                                   MERCE OF EGYPT

and the book to close with KNOWING ALL WAYS, INCLUDING THE
                                TRANSPOSITION OF CONTINENTS, which ends:

     America, Europe, Asia,
     I have no further use for you: your clamor
     divides me from love
     and from new noises

Cid—   You see?   All the biz. has got me off my arse.   Now I don't care
       what comes, hell or high water!   (All I have to do now is type!)
       But I hope nothing comes but a handsome book!   (For after sitting
                              down to such funeral baked meats,
                              I crave hornpipes from the printers!

Don't, in any case, let anything take any of your pleasure away from the
venture too!
        Let me hear——*all*

WE'RE OFF!!

      Hoo-   Amore
ray!

sat nite

cid:
       a fast note, to tell you yr letter of 13th was in my hands
last night—BUT (the mails are so nutty) Creeley's letter to me
on MSS (problem of sect 4 etc etc) only came in here before supper
tonight!
            (a 4 day differential between Boston and here!)

       Anyhow: decided a cable was called for.   Which went off

an hour ago saying:

                         On Book trust you completely STOP Therefore
                         Section 4 out STOP All thanks and luck

For he sure did sound grim!   (Have just dropped him additional note

saying, lift, lad, the point of this is the three of us not lose

the lustre.   (Told him i had note fr you saying to me ok ok ok.   And I

was passing it on to him: ok ok ok.)

. . . So: it ends on LA CHUTE.   And that, I think, is a happy thing of it
all too.   (Why not, admit it?)

And the page breaks he sends us both is a sign of care & damned
good sense, don't you think?   (I checked those and they seem excep-
tionally good).

IN FACT, I think he seems to have cause to be less grim! and you

and I?   Well.   Yr letter to me was equally sound!

                              OK.   We're over there, being
                              printed, I guess, eh? . . .

cid—7 just in a half hr ago (but don't let my speed diminish in yr
mind the edge of my response: for i have the feeling this is all too
important for me not—at least, on yr own things—to give em the
carefullest work, so that you may begin to see what the task is

nor do i arrogate to myself anything you haven't given me in putting me
there ORIGIN so—and saying, he's . . . central . . .

for so much of all of this (I haven't read Benn's dialog, except to
sample it, and already despair, that a man who wrote MORGUE shld
not *know* the dialog is one of those forms only such stuffed birds as Valery . . .
just that use alone fits that cry of his that, Nobody's—Yrs (His): shit, it's

anyone's, not those hortations, expecially, NOT

that christly lie, (Lohner's) the po-et's—the POE-ETTES

                                        (it gets me how

a man who did MORGUE/doesn't get better

                                (and Enslin using the bar /
so falsely—that *valuable* thing: how can he be so cute
with public property . . .

        This is why I must tell you.   And tell you more (by the way of yr own
verse):
        SOMEWHERE (and it must, finally, be you—as yr verse can show)
USE, AND NOW, are getting—THIS ISSUE—
                                TOO FUCKING *ORGANIC*

                                (I wish I had caps as big as
                                 these words must go into
                                 YOU

TOO FUCKING DREARY AND

                        FLAT

                                (christ, arise, awake, and go alert!
                                 my son: use

that which man's got to replace his mitts, his

116

HEAD   (yrs,
                Benn's,
                          MINE   (it's my head feels

CHOPPED OFF—i go crazy thinking of
                    such a juxtaposition as
                                MISS rain in the twat—for chris-
sake, in origIN?

                    Nouns, and image:
                                god, corman, you must go to school
to ME: you must *take* it: you must LEARN

                                (example, the Red Oak. I do not
                                despair.   The fox skin isn't
                                bad.   But jesus: CID::::

it AIN'"T that EASY, bro., not at all, not   NOT   NOT   NOT

that easy

            Benn, likewise, in all that stuff (after HOLDERLING?
                                if that is what patmos is,
                                he (benn) shld
                                SHUT UP

These are SERIOUS THINGS
                    (I find myself not banging Enslin (that he has
                    some of the gift, not as much as benn in 1912,
                    but some:
                                but i bang you YOU for letting him
                    out SO SOON into

                    the *public domain:*

                                    as well, yr—

self (why not, when you have this citizen here, and say you value him, why

not let him go over you, dig you, say: cid,

there's MUCH

to be learned (for ex.,
                to write in quatrains, you better
                then
                behave   BE-
                HAVE: you better
                (learn how to)

                rime

arise,
and go to
school: hang that one
on this issue; 7
o'clock—and A
M, mind you, break-
fast, time
to milk the cows
FIRST—chores,
you damned pseudo-Su
merians

NO, cid.   I can't grant
this one
passage—passaje : I cry
NO Passaran!
                    And I cry it
fr the necessity to
KEEP PROPER
COMPANY!

                              (I'll be back on

with details, that is, I'll
be on yr
back, on
YOU, who

has got to get up!

It's altogether a question of being *Simpler*   *STRAIGHTER*

MORE MODESTY, all hands a-round!

                    (& as Chaplain sd
                    to the newspaper man:
                    "And simplest, my boy,
                    AIN'T simple."

cid:

　　　　now i've got you on my mind—that you've put yrself there—let
me keep filing the feelings as they come to me until such time as i can
get to that terrible task of hanging it all on where it comes from: the
lines and things of the verses

　　　　　　　　　　　　　　(((and do hold: it may be—as, e.g., it
　　　　　　　　　　　　　　was for RC/that only last week cid, i,
　　　　　　　　　　　　　　after an 8 months accumulation of his
　　　　　　　　　　　　　　poems in mss here, sit down and attack
　　　　　　　　　　　　　　it—do the job

　　　　for that sort of job is more difficult than to write verse
　　　　itself—much more (why, e.g., critique is such a thing to be
　　　　respected——and why it can't be done as it is almost exclusively
　　　　done in the public print, as reviews, or as introductions, or
　　　　all that shit—"critiques"—"criticism", that phoney trade

OK.　　The point is, to say this to you came to me as i walked along the
pond trying to find two stillson wrenches to take a stone Kate put down
the sink out:

　　　　why you can *hear* me is precisely the reason i cld sit
　　　　at yr table, and enjoy yr father, sister, mother, those
　　　　chops, and them—and you

　　　　you see, Cid, you do not write of, by, abt, for, in any way
　　　　CORMAN
　　　　　　　　　　and i know the reason: that it is the immensely diffi-
　　　　cult thing for any human being to do is: TO SPEAK OF ONE'S
　　　　SELF AND ONE'S THINGS
　　　　　　　　　　　　　　　especially us, us heteros of these
　　　　States & tenements, as I am, as you are, who

　　　　HAVE ONLY OURSELVES

you must cease instantly to think of a poem as anything but an expression
of THAT WITH WHICH YOU ARE A SPECIALIST—which has to be, if it is
a poem, YRSELF,　YR THINGS, no one else's, nothing else but that which you
are SURE of
　　　　　　　　and you must be prepared to find that you have LITTLE to speak of:
that, surprisingly enuf, is what we all find—that—as The Confuser sd—it's
all/as much/as on the back of/a postage stamp

　　　　　　　　　　　　　　　　CLEARLY, you are writing abt

what you think are the proper subjects of writing—not at all abt one, CID
CORMAN:
                    please *hear* me.   I am giving you a present.   It's
                    yrself.
                                We Americans have nothing but our personal details.
Don't let anyone fool you, any poet, any body.   There is nothing but all the
details, sensations, facts which are solely known to Cid Corman.   And
you must stick to them—get them straight—even if (AS IT DAMN WELL IS)
NOTHING. Understand? It will seem—does seem to you—NOTHING: that is

why you are writing abt anything everything but CORMAN. Because Corman to
Corman is ZERO.
                        what you don't know is, that that is as it is for anyone
                        but the pseudo-whatever:
                                    that we begin with ZERO—are O.

(If Lear sd zero, then believe him—for he was talking it straight—as
 a Shk will

            But you must forget Shk Olson Benn anybody BUT corman:

as it is it is all over corman's will, not corman

                            get me?

Just start fr scratch.   Write childlike, if you like.   Write like you don't
have any more right to use language than as, in the 3rd grade, they told
us that a sentence was a complete thought.   Make any sentence a complete
thot

and a paragraph—write it like the books say, not like writers now can't
write a paragraph (i mean those writers who show they have started from
scratch—did find out to begin is to begin with nothing—that big round
O which is only what we can honestly say is something we have known

You see, it shows instantly, whether a man is talking abt that which he
knows—or is talking abt what he wishes he knew

Cid, believe me (this is not at all—any of this—olsonism: it can't
be ducked by assuming i am talking some doctrine: I am talking the most
ordinary common (I think the word is) sense:
                                a man can only express that
which he knows

                    Now the further difficulty is, we think we know.   And that
                    too is a mare's nest: we don't even know until we bend
                    to the modesty to say we have nothing to say.   Then we offer

120

our *conjectures* abt what it is we have found to wonder abt:

that's what a poem is, a conjecture abt an experience we
are, for what reason, seized by—BUT I MEAN SEIZED.   It
has to be something on our mind, really on our mind, at
the heart of us—where it hurts

I promise you: the moment you say in verse a thing which registers on me
as a thing which sounds to me as tho it is where you hurt, I'll tell you,
quick.
          But you must start in: you must say, cid, begin with, cid—NOTHING
else

And i offer you this bait: IT IS WHAT YOU *WANT*! You actually want to be
a poet.   Well, take it fr me: any of us has to BEGIN.   And what I am telling
you is the beginning, IS THE BEGINNING.

And at the same time let me make you a promise: you won't be what you
want to be until you talk abt pork chops!
                              It ain't—and never was—any
different.

          Ok.   Sermon ♯2.

                    Ergo,

                              sum

Mon
Feb 2   (the day of the beginning of olson's eight-week stint of eight
          lectures plus, on, the new sciences of man, an Hinstitute
          culminating, the last three weeks with three others here,
          Christopher Hawkes, from England, author of "Prehistoric
          Fndts of Europe", Dr. Marie-Luise von Franz, associate of
          Jung fr Yurrup, and Robt Braidwood, fr Oriental Inst, there,
          Chi—and just back fr excavations Jarmo, and other sites,
          into earliest known towns of men, there, Iraq, Iran. . .

(the whole show's known hereabouts as—so Con tells me—"Olson's thing". . .

letter:

          Ho, ho, cid corman, on, olson being vague.   Ha-ha, as the other
          citizen sez: when the day comes i cut into a mss of cid core-
          man, wow!   You shld see the old man when he is after lines, images,
          the turnings of lines into each other and from same the emergence
          of that form we are still so foolish as to call a po-em!
                                                                    Ho!
          landsman!

but all such things must, now, give way to maps, charts, dates, arches,
dreams, origins, research, such stuff, such stuff!   For the next eight
weeks I shld be nobody's daddy
                              (my own stuff goes like this—tho no-
body will ever see these titles—the "legend" of a map won't be done
but shld be if the guy who knows silk screen process here weren't such
a neat shit:
                    The Cave, or, Painting
                      The Cup, or, Dance
                        The Woman, or, Sculpture
                          The Valley, or, Language

                    The Plateau, or, the Horse, or, War
                      Lagash, or, the Hero
                        Thebes, or, the City
                          The Sun, or, Self

A feller, name's Creeley, is very busy over there, I gather, what?

                              OK   keep coming

122

CID!!!!!!!!
        to TELL you
               WHAT A THING IT IS
                        to give you all: THANKS!!!!!!

for i think (fondly) the BOOK is beautiful—can't get over what a job
the lad did the 1st time he took such a task in hand
                        by god, almost
perfect:
        and the point is, it wldn't a been had not you sd, let it
be: i am full of that rejoicing as well

                        (I read the things last night,
as the last session of this damned institute—enclosed will give you
some clue to what i have been up to, and why i had to be off the hook
so long—do excuse it, please
                    (above squash is Kate's, who plays a
new game—holding on to the carriage of the machine!
                           we have pictures
of her to send you & the folks, but we can't find the damn things! will
tho

and the type, and the page, reads like cream (i think Robt is rite, when
he sez, it's human, that book, feels like humans made it

It just is the greatest, like they say—that is, the book, O ♯8.   Am
in a dream.   OK.   To tell you, and, to tell you!
                      All the biggest pleasures
              for yrself too in it

Cid—

    Been involved in a run of 4 new Max's (provoked by Ferrini's
4 whatever they ares)

    Done today.   So now it's only a question of final mss of all eight
(fr yr ♯1, thru 8) to be published Stuttgart (I may have told you, with
                                  Gerhardt, as printer–designer)
by a fellow named Williams:
    The Maximus Poems
title: 1–8   Will see you get carbons
                                     of the new ones (did you
                                     have a look at ♯4, "The
Songs, of Maximus"?)

    And then I'll be able to tell you again what a damned big
pleasure O8 was, is, shld be for several & sundry
                               (keep a flock for
the BMC citizens; they want to buy)
    And to tell you your mother shld have seen Kate in those
green toweling pajamas!   She looks like something of the Commedia
del Arte (very beautiful—much more so than in a plain long nightshirt!)

    OK.   Just to keep us on.
                                    (These new Maxies rough up Vinc
considerably—I was shocked by both the choice of things, & their
putting together
                    (to put chowder before a Maximus—or at least such
a one, as that one, ♯3!!
                         But this is only a part *of the bigger wrong.*
Hold his hand (tho I don't think he deserves forgiveness)

I just hate
that the necessities (at least as I take them
are bigger
than we are
          only hate it, that he had to go & get caught in the wringer

cid:

    that's old Pop-off for you, eh?

                   (in fact,
not at all obliged to him, to hear it is
at least an improvement on, the usual, silentia
of the appearance of oneself, before

THE PUBLIC

        (what gets me—each time—is how Bill
suddenly trots out a vocabulary which has been in
the attic, sometimes:
           it puzzleth me.

"with some work", he says.   Or something.   Well,

that, it seems to me, is where i do ride up.   And so,

the inevitable he's looking for, isn't

there   (I'm

slippery . . .

   PS: the funniest thing is, Preface—from inside
        the maker of em all—is the one has, for
        sd maker, the lack of
        GIMP!

           Thus it's the last one
        I'd be likely to
        imitate!

           Let me hear, back

Cid
     I've been slow, this summer, actually too much going on
here for the likes of me, *Ponderosa Americana*!
                              But yr note in, &
Miss Avison's finely drawn words (which, may I keep, for a couple of
days?), arouse me.
                    What I did do, was read 1-10 of Max one Sunday
night, & 11-22 the next Sunday.   And it taught me (at least, that *the
performing* of verse takes as much care as David Tudor, here, gives
to playing sd piano so magnificently that if you ever hear he's Boston,
catch his concert.)
                    Exactly where I am on that poem I am not sure. . . .

     Also, I cannot recommend to you & to Vigee too strongly, the idea
of getting a piece for ♯11 from *Pierre Boulez*, the composer (to whom
I shall inscribe the poem "Cold Hell"—to his Deuxieme Sonate—when—
as it wasn't the past time—an inscription is possible).   For Boulez is
one of the singular men alive.   And any thing he says is worth listening
to.   (If Vigee is not in touch with him there, I can take steps to ask
Boulez to let you have a piece.   Or, better, get you his address, Paris,
and you dig him, direct.   (Though all his writing known to me is on
composition, yet even that is instructive to the other arts, including
writing.   And he is so aware of form problems, that he could as well
do you, direct, from the base of music, a witty, sharp piece on
"the Creative" as of now. . . .

Keep me on.   And many many thanks for yr news—& Miss Avison!

el cid:
         did it (and wish i'd put in carbon, so that you might read too!
For it rolled out like a carpet!   And was a pleasure to do.   For I found
yr project excellently put.   And had the opposite of trouble pointing out
the pertinence of yr achievements to it.   In fact added a note saying flatly, that this was one of those times a recommendation was all gravy—that
I cldn't see how a man more joined to a plan as you & it.
                                          Wove it around
you, Origin, & yr instinctive wide & international "exchange".   In fact
got some such plug as this in: that you have made Boston what it has
not been for a very long time in literary & cultural affairs: the hub it
used to pride itself upon being!
                              And though (between us) I think you, as
well as all of us New Englanders (the Creel, the Black—who burns my
arse, the Lynn Fish, and those I do not know enough to call them
names (Eigner, the Cape Cod lad, etc.) that all of us are only parts
of a Landsgeist which has now, again, reasserted itself. . .
                                                     (note:
spelled it out most recently reading the mss of an ex-Air Force strut
fr Trenton (Pronounced "Trunnon") N.C., when I sd, if you study narrative with me; you will have to discover that certain New Englanders have
exposed the local (which has made Southerners the only successful story
tellers for 20 years—in fact, since Hemingway wrote "After the Storm",
the end of the national sociological school of the previous 30 years)—
they have exposed the local by demonstrating that the particular is a
syntax which is universal, and that it can not be discovered except lo-
cally, in the sense that any humanism *is* as well place as it is the person, that another of Socrates' crimes (who was improperly punished) was,
that he did give polis its death blow when he cried, Be, a Citoyen, du
Monde, that just this again is one of the Greek things which we late
citizens of Boston & environs—of the Geometric Culture (the houses,
even the three-deckers, yrs, and mine, Worcester; the wharves; the
mills; the Common; rocks, birds, difficulties; the plate glass, which
must be shattered)—have shattered
                              that dialect, is out of business, as
well as one world is, as politics, also being undone by the Hub
of
the
Universe

         OK, citizen.   A pleasure.

         As to our going matters, please excuse my apparent delays: tho
I have had to put my weight behind the College just at the moment (to
open it anew, and drive it toward some long (at least 3-yr) plan, the real
thing is that I have been lost in a quandary about the Maximus poem since

I wrote you that letter abt such problems of a long poem in June, was it?

And it has been a heady thing, to try to lick it—to see where (as I felt
I had) I had got off its proper track (with ♯24, and through ♯33).   And
it has meant the hardest sort of both wandering away and cutting it.   But
the upshot has been happy.   And tho I haven't been able (due to the recent
push to throw in, with the College) to write the new batch—probably another decade of 'em, one is already done, called Letter X, simply, that when
I did write it (two weeks ago) I hadn't, then, seen the path forward.   But
I did, last Saturday.   And the moment things lift a little, I should be able
to move it off its arse.
                                Not that there has been any drag.   Actually, as I
think i must have told you, 11-23 got solid in August, and are sitting
for final mss the moment I hear fr Williams that he is ready to make Book
♯2. . . .

Oh yeah!   Craziest thing of all!   —that recent researches all on
"*Dorchester*" !!!!
                                If there is an old bookstore near you, do keep yr eye
out for any stuff on settlement of yr town, especially *Roger Clap's
Memoirs*, 1844 (one of the first settlers).
                                                Much obliged.

(They sailed to Boston Bay in the *Mary & John*, 1630——anything on the
vessel, too.   Also an earlier group of 40, in 1629, on the Lyon's Whelp!)

You—
        who have never come to grips with any place—or person

   to be that much
a part of—what is
there! *that* situation   even a
not the isolated   lead leaf
                fort.   has more
                                                  life *in it*.

this is reason
the drag of
one line on
another—   rephrase—
going
        on   to get on   the voyage *out*
                  with it   is the voyage
                                                              in

Cid! . . . much involved with act of: NOUN, how it is not handle
but properly tail—that one shld have to work one's way thru anything
(any person) BEFORE. . . that the KNOWN shld precede noun.   Whereas,
it is what comes ahead, and so, we are so swift, we take the name as. . . .
and so hinder just what the real is, what we don't know until it is,
known.

     That the "shift is substantive", as Creeley tells me I do say in
letter 5 of the Mayan Ls.

     Nor is this, i suspect, what it might look like,
what WCW was after, in GRAIN.   I suspect Bill's nominalism is so
thorough he lost his game—at least that *after* Grain the nominalism
stayed fixed.   And thus he went the opposite path fr that one which Grain
showed him.   Or anyone.   To the Pelasgians.   (It is a huge error, imposed
on Bill in review of Koch by G. Smith in last NMQ, that Bill's ethic was
Emerson's self-reliance.   Wrong wrong wrong.

     in fact such a shame
(and on Crane & Pound too) that i have written my 1st letter to the Times!
To Lash, two pages, exposing, this Smith.   Hope he'll print it, so you
see it.

     That is, if i think EP gave any of us the methodological clue:
the RAG-BAG; bill gave us the lead on the LOCAL

     Or put it that pat:
EP the verb, BILL the NOUN problem.   To do.   And who, to do.   Neither
of them: WHAT.   That is, EP sounds like what, but what his is is only
more methodology, in fact, simply, be political.   Politics—not economics—
is him.   And validly.   For (1) politics is a context as wide as nature, and
not only what we call "politics"; and (2) its essence is will.   Which latter
—will—is what EP cares abt.   And why he hates dramah: that it is the
alternative of act in art to politics (dran, to do.   Will contradicts tragedy,
insists upon cause & effect in the face of stupidity (which is so close to
"life" that one can call it either way (that is, if one is Pound!   And Bill's
what, at heart, isn't any more than (no matter how much he damn well is)
than, Bill—as much as he does make it possible for any man to breathe
himself in like manner.   That is, Bill's dispensation is a hell of a lot
closer simply that he don't think it's stupid.   (I sd it, in "Grandpa, Goodbye",
as Bill fire to P's light—literally, light, the physics, of same, thus not
love (as Guido) but will (Ep's poems are—after the early Guido's—one
long extrapolation, canzone, on WILL: how, to get it, up.   And the image:
"process, . . part of, the, process" (proceeding, progress, advance,
change, hope, the. . . BLAST, instead of the STORY (no, drama, please,
to-DAY, no sire, PLAY. . . . . . . Only, Bill didn't stoke, sd fire.   Which i
am sure was backward from, sd Sam Houston or / Eeeerick (in fact Bl
says it, in Sam, how, he goes down.   Only Bill wldn't also see down as
out.   Great guys, that they still make it so much one can say, only—
NO WHAT   (??)

                Lawrence, the
              real   one as
            one

Cid: you are immodest.   And thus you do outrage another man.

Or maybe
this is rage, at having maximus measured outside itself.   And i shld fall back
on what i have sd to you before, that you are not at home to yourself, are
not simply simple, as any man is who looks after his self.

For you impose
on me a hierarchical system which is only yr own, is no part of my life or
work.   (In fact, I read exactly the passage you put between the Pat quotes
& the Cant as *distinct* from either.   And that makes me feel very damn good,
thank you.

But i don't feel good abt you.   For you don't, obviously, see that.   You see
something else—a necessity to say something abt a disappointment of yr own
in it.   Which, of course, is, flatly, yr own behindhandness—that Pound &
Williams are yr measure of music, not the moving music of other men.   And
which—any of us who are now singing—is not at all involved in any
such value comparisons.   What they did is there.   What we do, is.   That's
all

I just damn well don't like the establishing of *relations*.   They are phoneys.
And are dodges, for finding out, what is *relevant* inside any given thing.   To
itself.

Christ, to say i leave the music in the things!   You, who have seen
that it was published!   And now, by god, you use the very virtu of the practice
to mouth WCW and Eppie at me, as, superior.   Fuck em, even if they are.
It's none of our bizness.

Or at least it ain't, between the two of us.   You
at home, maximus, at home.   That's the combo.   And on the toilet seat,
if you must be, that factual.   I don't give a damn.   I'd rather you were on
a toilet seat and shitting—than in this high chair you think (and say Creeley
can't sit in) that criticism is.

Forget criticism.   It's a phoney, too—a
fraud you are practicing on yrself.   And thus on Origin.   Let me let out all
the stops.   I was fucking sore, the way you put Morning News *last* in that
issue.   And not at all because WCW was first.   But because the poem—
and by yr own original editing principles, "to compose, the magazine"—
patently (and just because it does read, End broadcast, end poem) belongs
no where but first, to make any sense out of its publication at all.

And of course the reason why it was where it is is, now you say it, that
you honestly,—finally—do feel that older names must be somehow, better
music.

Shit, Cid.   Excuse me.   But come on in.   Come off the high-chair
(which is, precisely, its proper name.

Come out among men, where they are—
and not, for christ sake (where's yr head?) where Mr. Williams sez they are

most alive, when they are dead!   Good god, merely read what's sd.   And
don't so fucking much worry abt what you are going to say abt what you have
read.   it ain't written to be criticized.   It is written to be read, that's all.
(Doesn't that occur to you? . . .
                              (In fact,—again, to let out a stop—this
bizness of writing poems on the poems of other men (me, Bill, Benn);
and
        writing critiques, for "Poetry"!
                              Shit.   Just shit.   I say again:

write abt Corman.   His things.   And live like that.   And at the same time
don't exaggerate yr generosity: the fine—the damn fine thing abt you is,
that you are generous, you do go out of yr way for others (ex., Olson: for
christsake, look what you have done for sd Olson, by publishing him, by
creating a magazine where he can be read

                                      but that's it.   Why think yr generosity
has to restrict itself?   Contract to criticisms?   Why not leave it be—as the fine
thing it is?
        (What will, to destroy, leads you to think you are more than
generous?   what unhappy desire requires you to be significant?

                                              If you were
as simple as I choose to enjoy you as, you wld wear yr generosities for themselves—as you wld read olson's work.   For itself.   Not for comparison to
two now holy cows,
                two now wholly acceptable
                                      measures

No cid.   I blast you, because you must wake up.   You won't move (which is
what you honestly must want.   So long as you fuss up yr nature by such roles
& false necessities

                (for gawd sake simply read that creeley statement.   and join
                it to yr own observation that i leave the music in the
                things themselves
                              and then ask yrself where is yr crying
                me down by way of those two mahsters
                                              —where is, not in
                words, but in things?

                (ha-ha

OK.   Burn.   But not merely this occasion, bro.   Don't think I am that petulant.

I know what's missing in the music.   But it's olson which ain't there, not
Williams or Pound.   And you shld know that's who is missing.   Not these
two inferior predecessors—just as I am inferior, to myself! and predecessor, of myself!

        I am not one to keep after a man.   But you will recognize this
        letter as having inferior predecessors—at least two, one last
        year on Origin, a penny post card; and another, three years
        ago, on the whole biz of how such a mag might live

                                                So take
        this as another keynote.   And don't assuage yrself I merely
        swing back.

        I watch you.   And when I am roused I tell you.

                                        And now
(because it is late, and we are either more close, or it isn't much of a game)
I come in closer: you be quiet.   Or you won't know.
                                I sd wake up, a year
ago.   I say, jack up, now.
                        It's more serious, because both of us are more
disclosed.   And Maximus, is a fair test, bro.
                        Love

132

Cid:

i'm a hot one.   And you sure cooled me, with those two, the one on
the reading Gloucester (which got a letter out of Helen, she, too, cool &
gracious); and yr last, with no rebuke for, me jumping all over, you, and
you only saying wot was yr thot

i just have to demand of you, special,
simply, that you have been so much my friend

And i also hereby cause
you pain, of another sort.   I don't know abt yrself, but it has taken me 40
yrs to find out that one has to cause those one is closest to, pain—and still
i can't do it, have no guts for it, was raised without it, and still haven't
caught up with the way the rush of life does do exactly that.

The point is, i
hope i am the first to tell you that Robt is coming here as of March 29th,
not only as an addition to the faculty in writing, but as editor of a new quarterly,
to be called "The Black Mt. Quarterly", 100 pages, big review section, and
planned to compete with Kenyon, Partisan, NMQ (what else is there, are
Hudson, & Sewanee, still in existence?).   Anyway, that sort of thing.   And
with a circulation of 2500 to be shot at.   Also, to carry ads.

I have been so
damned caught up in a mailing of the announcement of the new faculty for
March 29th; plus an appeal for 250,000 bucks, for expansion (and, for that
matter, to float this mag); plus another fund drive for same amount, to be
a series of three, to come at the same time as the first issue of the quarterly
(April 1st), three programs NY, a concert directed by Mitropolos, a show
by Kline, Dekooning, Tworkov, Vicente, Guston (the space cadets, who have
all been here the past two years); and a performance by Merce Cunningham's
dance company—all to be the kick off of the fund drive

—that i have been kept from this letter to you.

Anyhow, there the damned
betrayal is—or so pain to such as yrself always strikes me, as.   And i want
you to feel very damned free to dump me like a hotcake, if you wish: that is,
if you are so sore you want to cut me to hell out of Origin like that (in other
words, want to call off all that I am making up for you for ♯12) why just damn
well poke me in the puss.

I hope to christ you don't.   As   I figure it   this
is a mag of another order.   And will catch us all into itself, as well as a lot
of ginks Origin wldn't have bothered with—as Bob plans it, he wants a very
wide base, so it won't fall on any small number issue after issue, nor be one
man's headache. . .

ok.   that's it.   that's the bad news.   And of course, on the
other face, it's terrific: that the College is willing to take it on, try it,
seek the dough to support it.   And I, of course, am damned glad Robt does
get this chance to pull off what—as he says—he twice planned, and didn't effect.

He's it.   And i'm sure you'll hear from him.   Me, i'm just the culprit, or so
i feel, so far as you are concerned—and no damn other person whatsoever. . . .

                        A very damn great letter in yesterday, from
Gloucester, i want you to see—from the man who owns the house with the
Bullfinch doors!   Just the nicest sort of word a man might hope for, from,
the town!

. . . Let me now try to find yr two recent letters, among the piled up mail of
the last weeks.   This, to you, is the very first one i have got to—and
will try to start cutting away at it, with this word to you.

                                    ((Just reread
Avison letter . . . Miss A is very damned good there, on the *lateral* vs
upsidedownumbrella (it is one of the reasons—that is, my own desire
to pass on to something else—why i have been dragging my foot on the
2nd PV piece for you we talked of).   I, of course, wld not think Yeats'
gyre is the alternate.   On contrary.   It's down the whorl would be, screwed,
you might say.   But her protest is one i had taken to my own position
(perception. . . . it was only to insist upon speed.   And drive.   Instead
of the very thing she speaks of, which (in others than herself i am damned
sure) got pretty tedious.   And dead. . . .

134

MY dear CID:
            just to give you the greetings
of, this yr, and—the ONE, a-HEAD!

And to tell u again i read a pome of yrs today
with plai-
sir
        and not the french of apollinaire, BUT

yr own, there, on -o,
fee-
us

        (not thinking the subject straight on can
        be, re,
        investigated
                    that it is too lost in cli-
che,)
        but very much thinking yr line is showing

with 'em!

            And to hail it.   And to ask, for,
more!

        Still crazy stuck with the need of this
place for dough (in spite of plans!

And so haven't moved a jot.   But will get you
those poems, say, N Y Day—to meet, yr, deadline

        And for the flip, enclose, sd latest pub-
lication of, this, Collitch: off press yesterday

and me mailing all night, and now again, after

posting this to you.   That done, all i have to

do is write a statement for Alfred Einstein to
make, saying, Black Mt is Black Mt is Black Mt
i mean Black, folks
                and i'm thru—free, for, my
own affirs.

My dear Cid ! ! ! ! !
                    Finally.   And all pardons.   Simply, that, this Quarter,
this place fell on me.   And there was nothing to do but make the push: to
see, if, somewhere, we might, break through, get dough, operate, find
an Advisory Council, make possible more students (the Korean Bill, etc.)
—and such a "center" as the mag, books, etc. might make it.   You will
see how, in these States, knowing yr own attack, what it is to make same!

                    (By the way, along that path, Huss asked me
yesterday: wld you, in this one instance, give us a chance to grab a
chance last student or two for the summer quarter—starting in a couple
of weeks—by loaning us yr mailing list to send out to it the Summer
Bulletin, announcing a "writing institute" ? ? ? ?
                                        I sd I didn't like to ask
a man for his life-line, but that I thought you wld, because you "started"
us all by magazine, in this one instance let us "load" the list.
                                        But you must
judge whether you favor letting the mailing list carry a "college" item.
                                                        If you
can, Huss wld be terribly grateful.   For the burden of getting the mechanics
done, is on him.   And "distribution"
                        is where we stay pitifully
                                        WEAK!

(I can't myself stand it much longer.   Either we lick this mailing list biz
(plus dispatch of goods along the same line of communication, like the
Review, plus any books, etc.) or we better give up.   I had hoped Jonathan
wld cut in here.   But he is a "publisher" not a marketer.   And you know
Creeley and myself.   And the College has been limping along with a 5000
name list which is—so far as I can see—as dead as the Old College was
five years ago/
                    You will know how seriously I take this "marketing" biz: all
of our several publishing ventures—and I mean of such things as education,
as well as Origin, and books (Contact, Civn, poems, Max, etc.)—are
playing in sand boxes unless they are attacking on the distribution level.

It's a damn nuisance, and not what active men are likely to give their
attention to.   But I swear if each of us *did his own* that the pool wld eventually
catch up with the possible fact.
                        (Example: Maximus.   Damn it.   So far as
I can find out the sales were chiefly from that list of my own "friends".   This
is crazy.
                    Tho, godhelp us, I myself rest the case ahead: that is I think yr
♯12 is going to make a difference.   (By the way, when ? ? ? ?
                                        Can't tell
you how anticipatory I am abt that one!

. . . Crazy, to have Creeley here.   Crazy, that we never talk (in any large
sense).   It's great: all fast, like telegrams.   And what a contrast to the
volubleness when we are 500 miles off!
                                    5000

     But I suppose what's on my heart today is the sense of yr proximities,
And they pull, now, to Bristow—if you get what I mean.   That is, Maximus
pulls you, for me, toward Gloucester!
                                        And so you are in my heartland!
                        How are things, there?   (I mean with
you.
                    ((Info: I am back at the MONSTER.   Or so it became over
                        the past year.   Simply, that I had to reattack.   It got lost,
                        somewhere in the '40s.   And I had to find my way back on
                        my own path.   As well as its path.
                                                feel now I have: a
                    spate of new ones done.   But also—and this was the break-
                    through—altogether non-Maximus poems.   Crazy.

                    Please keep writing me.   Miss the news, and going of your
own concern.   Plus the old "family" of us.
                                        (It's like Creeley getting here.
Seems to have cut off, the old wild play!)

137

My dear Cid!
          I love you very much, & I would arouse you from
just the giving too much to the world as it is what you give me back
for my piece on the theater in the first letter from you there,
Europe—specifically, Paris, that *old* metropolis—just in.

          Look, Cid; be sure (1) that I have long gone over,
& finally discarded, all those possibilities you think, because
they *ought to*, those media now current as theater offer (theater,
film, radio, TV).   And the thing wipes out all your self-evidents
is simply, *ownership*;
                    & (2), that if any one of us did real
theater—& I submit what I sd there, how only it can be done
(as, for example, in his form, DHL did it, because he had the
passion for tragedy)--then those media will come-a-running
(as they ran after, in the end, when he was dying, Thomas).

          You'll not find any light in how those media are/
any more—& think of this! ——than you know yrself the
politics of the world (ownership uber Alles) yields any possibility
to the individual man as passionate creature.

          So *please*, go back & read it *after* yr letter, imagining
that I have been through it all—even TV, by god, Washington, 1950.
And even radio, *Boston*, 1937!

          And Cid—please always forgive me any harshness, like
I think you may find my review of yr Eclogues.   It is never the back
of my hand.   It is that passion, that all things be done right.   And take
it, please, that I wouldn't talk back if I didn't *love*!
                              And happened to pay
attention just because it was you!

          All love, & keep me on to yrself, etc. / the Best thing
was the END!
          And I thank you, from the heart.

My dear Cid (Aug 24, 1955—Thank you for your letters, & the newest
Origin.   And maybe the turn has come, and I shall seem like a correspondent friend supporter: there is the solidest chance yet that, in a very few
days, we may have managed the sale of 200 acres—and be off again on
the pursuit of the gleam of the place: that is, we will have a chance
to proceed forward without every day having to make the ends meet.   For
two years flat—and one and one half years without any salary—we have
had to go forward without knowing when the next foot might fail.   Now
it looks as though we will have a different problem: we will have a year
and a half with at least the College taken care of/and during that year
and a half we will have to raise the money (actually not money but students,
or, the equivalent of them, scholarships at $550 a head: 43 of them, in
18 months, or, 3 per month, or, $1650 per month!

So keep up the good work.   Tell any guy who has $550 he can come here
and get tuition and rent (and food he can live on at the rate of what he
can eat himself; and with four months winter to raise that little bit to
feed himself by).   Several, by the way, have written from the Boston
area, but none of them yet (except the two who were at the Charles St.
Church that night of Hazel, and came in off the street, John Wieners and
Joe Dunn) have got here.   But the point is, the time in which that work
of Origin etc will count is in the next 18 months.

So I feel a little bit better, maybe.   And will probably take the Fall
Quarter off, leaving Creeley to fend off the characters here.   —I am
hoping, in fact, to get to New England.   Will you be back, or no?   What
are yr plans ? ? ? ? ?

                       . . . I think you will be pleased to hear that I did get
MAXIMUS II done in July—and it is already at Stuttgart, in Dr. Cantz'
Druckerei.   It will be about the same length as I, even tho it has 2 more
letters, that is, it is 11-22, I think.

And it leaves me faced with III (or whatever form the next one will take,
probably a single volume of all—whatever:
                                        crazy to have that space
staring me in the face!   And though I think I know what fills it, the act
of doing it is more than I can say!   Or do.   Instead, I do what the day
presents.   It is too much, broken up as things are here, to set in, at
present, to that push.

My dear Cid
              Coming / finally / up for air
                              Had so much time to make-up
for
      Wild thing is that, since before yr previous letter, have been preparing
a thing for you:
              THE SPECIAL VIEW OF HISTORY
                                      & in hope I cld finish it
so that you might use it, if it struck you, for the final ORIGIN, simply

that it comes as the climax of—in order   1)   Gate & C
                                           2)   Escaped Pants
                                           3)   Apple Loner   ?
                                           4)   HU
                                      &   5)   it

as so a book, but if not, there in the file of O the whole. . .

          Wonderful to have yr news and please keep it coming at me—I
pray I shall be a better correspondent once again from here out:

does look as tho i might, for the struggles of the last 2 to 3 years are

OVER !. !!!

140

Cid—
        forgive.
                The thot of having missed Origin 20 is unbearable.
But above all to have you there thinking I fouled out.   Wow!   A damn
mean thing for me not to be there.
                        Got caught in the folding of this
place.   It was the last days—& I had to see it through (this is for you:
officially we are "closed for improvements"! (I'm to stay to do the
"improvements"—but it's for sale!
                        Alas, soon as I paint a few
buildings, I'll be back on my own bucket—but it comes too late, I
feel sure, to catch you.   If by any chance, you do have room in any
last forms, *cable* me *collect* & I'll damn well *do* something.
                                This
at least quickly to register written chagrin—& to ask yr indulgence
(3 yrs of this place (where it was rough) is now *over*.   I shld be
back among the living.
                All best to you
                    & *yrs*

                        Charles Olson

141

I have worked to edit these letters according to the principles which they propose. Thus a primary concern has been to respect, absolutely, Mr. Olson's spelling, spacing, and punctuation—to reproduce, as completely as possible, the original heat.

But as the text continued to strike its way into me, I became aware that to simply reproduce the entire mass of material with whatever scholarly clarifications (as I have done in the form of a doctoral dissertation for the State University of New York at Buffalo) did not answer the final demand of the text I so much respected. Rather, the task became one of seeing clearly that bounding outline already present in the mass and of bringing it out, visible, for public view. And so, like a Cro-magnon hunter in the dark recesses of a cave, I began to stare at these surfaces, page by page. I began to make careful exclusions (indicated by ellipses) and to include missing details (always enclosed in square brackets), until the creature I had been hunting appeared to me in an entirety not my own.

> *These songs are called the sweat house*
> *songs. In them old man, old woman,*
> *& single man refer to the sun, moon*
> *and morning star. The timber refers to*
> *the smudge stick.*

Albert Glover
Canton, 1969

31-100